Dear God! I Never Wanted To Be A Salesman!

To Marie ~
Very best wishes
& every success!

04/02

Dear God! I Never Wanted To Be A Salesman!

The Best of Tim McMahon

From the Pages of "The Value Proposition"

Tim McMahon

Writers Club Press

San Jose   New York   Lincoln   Shanghai

Dear God! I Never Wanted To Be A Salesman!
The Best of Tim McMahon

Writers Club Press
an imprint of iUniverse, Inc.

For information address:
iUniverse, Inc.
5220 S. 16th St., Suite 200
Lincoln, NE 68512
www.iuniverse.com

ISBN: 0-595-22268-4

Printed in the United States of America

For Dad–who loved every story, understood exactly what it was all about, and knew more about selling than I ever will. It should have been your book…

Winners know there is always one more thing you can do…

CONTENTS

PART III
ON VALUE SELLING!

PART IV
SOME OLD YANKEE WISDOMS 'N SUCH!

FOREWORD

I truly love sales! I've been doing it now for thirty years as a sales rep, sales manager, and entrepreneur. I wasn't a "natural" by a long shot but I became very good at it. It was going to be a temporary thing–a way to get started in business–but instead it became my life. I'm only bitter occasionally.

I bet you're reading this because you too never wanted a career in sales. But somehow you're here, selling, and trapped like a rat! Now don't bother denying it because we both know better, don't we? They sucked you in just like they did me–it was only going to be for a little while and then you could move on to something you really wanted to do. Or did they say, "Everyone in our company starts in sales"? It doesn't matter now though–for better or worse, no matter what your job or title, in your heart you are A SALES REP!

Since we're both stuck in this selling thing I suppose we're left with no alternative than to be really great at it. One thing I have learned about sales is that it's only fun when you're really, really good. Being average or mediocre just doesn't cut it.

By the way, I don't believe that outrageous sales success has a lot to do with sales techniques. I know that's heresy and all the sales trainers will have conniption fits, but that's what I believe! Maybe you've mastered the "Nine Alternative Closing Techniques", know how to build instant rapport, and can "pre-close" with the best of them (and more power to you), but those are just not the skills that make the real top performers. Outrageous sales success comes from…well, you'll just have to read the book to find that out! And when your done, email me at **tim@mcmahonworldwide.com** to let me know whether you agree or not!

Sales and the whole business of selling and managing have changed so much over the last thirty years. We live in a new world, a new century, where all the rules and assumptions are changing daily. Customers have new expectations, buying patterns are different, technology in the form of the internet and tools such as CRM are refashioning the fundamentals of how we do our jobs. But Change creates Opportunity—as the sales landscape changes there are great opportunities for smart salespeople to create unique competitive advantage for themselves.

Over the years I have written hundreds of articles for sales magazines around the world and three books on "the new business of selling". In 2000 I became the publisher of "The Value Proposition", a sales e-magazine that reaches thousands of salespeople in over 25 countries. I hope that you will enjoy this collection of what I think are the best of them and that you will find ideas that will help you create your own "Outrageous Sales Success"! Worst case, I think you'll enjoy hearing why I never, ever wanted to be a salesman and how I found Success.

- Tim McMahon, March 2002

ACKNOWLEDGEMENTS

Sales is about the lessons you learn along the way. Sometimes it's from a book or listening to a great sales speaker. Other times it's from the advice and counseling of a mentor, a coach, or an especially good manager. There are also the incredibly painful lessons…but if I acknowledged all of them we'd be here all day. So perhaps it's enough just to thank some of the folks who taught me so much and encouraged me—despite my lifelong desire to *never, ever be a sales rep!*

It always begins and ends with Sue. For 30 years of marriage she's given me unerring (if occasionally painful) advice, insight, and most of all the support and confidence I needed. More than my spouse—my very best friend in the entire world! Each book is really *her* book…and I am still eternally grateful!

Jonathan Narducci, friend extraordinaire and co-publisher of "The Value Proposition", who still challenges *everything* I say but makes me the better for it…and Linda (no, I didn't forget this time!)

Paul Rayment, who taught me the most. Chris Heide, who first let me write. IBM who gave me the start; DEC for the opportunity to try!

And good friends, just for being good friends and good ideas—Vance Pool, Rob Mould, Jack & Linda Lockhart, Ken & Diane Asai, Bob & Meg Hamm…

And of course, the "Kids" who still aren't sure exactly what it is I do but they know it's always been for them—Casey, Katie, Tim, and Betsy. I'm proud of each of you!

PART I

DEAR GOD! I NEVER WANTED TO BE A SALESMAN!

DEAR GOD! I NEVER WANTED TO BE A SALESMAN !

Dear God, I never wanted to be a sales rep. I'm not kidding; I *really, really, really* never wanted to be a sales rep. Anything but that. I tried (oh, how I tried!) to be something else, but I was cursed.

I come from a long, long line of successful sales*men* (well, they were all men!). My Dad, like his father, was and an absolute master of the craft. He always encouraged me towards "the great profession". "Son, it's the best job in the world!" And like I said, I tried…he lied.

When I was nine years old I sent in a coupon from the back of a comic book to sell flower and garden seeds door-to-door. (You remember the ad, right?) In return for selling just a zillion packets for 25 cents each I would earn a brand new English Racer bicycle. Even if I only sold *half a zillion* I could get a radio controlled racing car…or a FlexiFlyer sled, or…well, you get the idea. I got lots of good stuff—well, I *would* have gotten lots of good stuff if I'd sold any seeds. It's now thirty-something years later. My mother may have thrown away my baseball card collection, but she's still got enough packets of those damn seeds up in the attic to re-plant the entire Earth. (If you need any flower and garden seeds call her; she'll sell them *cheap*!) Does this sound familiar?

I also tried selling greeting cards, candy bars, and magazine subscriptions. About the same results. In case there's ever a major disaster, I feel good knowing my mother will have plenty of reading material, something to eat, she'll be able to write her friends, and plant a garden.

Following this early *sales trauma*, I made every effort to avoid a sales career. I started college as a psychology major, but I quickly realized that psychology could have way too much to do with selling. Next I tried journalism; better but the potential to *influence* people was still there. Finally in desperation I graduated as a biology major because what could be safer or further from sales? So imagine my utter devastation when I found that the IBM Corporation suddenly wanted to hire me...as a *salesman!* For God Only Knows What Reason, somebody way high up there in IBM had decided that science majors made the best computer salespeople. Did this make any sense? No, of course not, but it is true. I honestly believe today that it only happened because I was cursed at birth to become a salesman.

So for thirty years I've been a more than successful salesman. Over a quarter of a century selling and finally I must confess that I love it—and I have loved every single minute of it. You probably wonder what happened. First let me say I still hate making cold calls and have always had major telephone aversion. I stress out just thinking about quotas and "making the big bucks" isn't my number one goal. Getting the "midnight worries" isn't my idea of fun either.

I found out that there are things I do love and that sales is the only path to them...

- I like to *think.* I enjoy creating strategies and tactics and finding solutions.

- I like to be *challenged.* I like my skills and abilities to be stretched and stretched again.

- I like to *learn*—a curiosity to learn from every situation and the people I meet.

- I want to *grow*—to develop my personal skills and abilities, to be the best I can.

- I have a passion for *ideas.* When I have an idea or find a solution to a problem I want to communicate it to others

- I'd like to *make a difference*—to feel that someone else is more successful or his or her life is improved because of what I did. and I do like to *Win...*

I thought selling was a battle between me and a reluctant customer. I thought that winning sales was about manipulation and persuasion using "sales skills". I learned instead that selling, when it's done right, is all the things I love.

Each new day and each new opportunity is a challenge. To meet that challenge requires me to *think* and to *learn* from my customers, the people I work with, and just about everyone else—and when I do that, I *grow* as well. *Communicating* my ideas—my solutions—to a customer and having them understand and agree with me is the greatest thrill, especially when we can both see that I've *helped* that customer become more successful or meet a need. And *winning* is the big payoff!

Dear God, I confess I never wanted to be a salesman, but then again what else could I have done?

A PROFESSION FOR LUNATICS

Really? You really want to be a sales person? Why? Do you realize just how much stress, aggravation, and frustration there is in selling? That it's an emotional and ego roller coaster? Trust me, there have got to be easier ways to make a living! For some reason, however, some folks still want to go out and sell. They must be crazy!

Some people say they sell because sales is where the money is! Well, it may be true that salespeople make more money than the average bear. I often wonder, however, if, when you divide all that money by the actual hours of selling, preparing, thinking, and sweating, whether it works out to be all that much more than the minimum wage.

Now you might wonder just how come I'm coming down so hard on selling. Did I have a bad week? Lose a big deal? No, nothing so dramatic. I've just been thinking a lot about my 25 years of selling and have finally concluded that I must have been deranged when I started and I never got any better.

I really don't regret it (I think). I've had a lot happen to me, however, and I don't mean just the ups and downs of quota. No, I even once had a " prospect " actually take me hostage at gunpoint for a day. In his defense, the *was* a little upset that day and he thought I was from the CIA, coming to take him away. A natural mistake perhaps—in those days CIA and IBM guys like myself probably dressed pretty much alike, all gray pinstriped suits and "sincere" ties. When he realized that all I wanted to do was sell him a computer , well , he was eager to buy! I took the order although I don't think we ever booked it (some problem about installing a mainframe in a padded cell).

Just another relaxing day of selling! Are we having fun yet?…more in Part 2.

A PROFESSION FOR REAL LUNATICS

The lunacy continues…

In the interest of building that all-important customer relationship, I once went sailing with crazy people. I've long since blocked most of it from my mind, but the persistent memory lingers of taking water in 20-foot seas far, far from land. When I yelled over the wind and rain, " Shouldn't we call the Coast Guard on the radio?", my customer-captain screamed back, " Good idea! Have you got one?". When, only by the grace of God , we reached port late that night, he said, "That was fun! Tomorrow we sail back home!". (I called my wife, begged her to drive 3 hours to rescue me from this sailing madman, and sorrowfully explained—to my soon to be ex-customer—that I had to leave him because of a terrorist attack on my home…or something.) Sometimes it's important to just live to sell another day!

Did I mention my client who insisted we go Go-Cart racing together? I sacrificed three broken ribs for that deal…Or the customer who told me our deal depended on whether his horse liked me, the horse being, I assume, an outstanding judge of character or something. He bit me (the horse not the customer). Swell…

Of course there's all the mundane things that happen, hardly worth mentioning. Getting lost in New York at midnight; getting lost in Los Angeles at midnight; getting lost in Toronto at midnight, getting…Why is it that when you get lost at midnight its never in Beverly Hills?

Clearly no rational human being would want a career with this much "fun". Wouldn't it be far better to go to a nice, quiet job every day never having to worry that anything weird might happen? When you get home at night no one would bother you with pesky questions like " Did anything interesting happen to you today? Close any big deals? Anything exciting going on? " It seems a far more rational way to live than this silly selling business.

Personally, I'm ready to stop selling right now. Well maybe not right now. There's this client of mine who just called and wants to go skydiving this afternoon. He says that if I pull the ripcord closer to the ground than he does then I win his business…Sounds reasonable. Gotta go!

TALES FROM THE ROAD

Who came up with the term "Road Warrior"? I appreciate whoever it was because before that we were just "lonely salespeople".

Even after all these years my wife is still convinced that life on the road is the Big Party. Fine restaurants and beautiful people. I thought about this one night while dragging my suitcase of dirty clothes into an airport Marriott at 2:00 AM. I thought I got a nasty look from the desk clerk when I muttered "It just doesn't get any better than this.", but I suspect he'd heard it all before.

This hotel has 24 hr. room service. Good thing. It's not a luxury, it's a necessity. After all, traveling salespeople might need party munchies at any hour, right? (I order a cold roast beef sandwich and a glass of milk.) Actually room service—that perc of the "rich and famous"—really is a necessity, simply because no human being can be expected to survive on an airline dinner alone.

Speaking of airline food, I wonder who came up with those dry turkey sandwiches on rolls rejected as too small for anorexic gerbils.

"We can save a zillion dollars a year by serving these new 'deli dinners'!"

"Great, but won't the frequent flyers complain?"

"Nah, we'll throw in a packet of Grey Poupon and call it gourmet!"

"Wow, you're a genius!!"

I'm looking forward to tomorrow night. I arrive early at my next hotel (if my flight's on time). I might even go down to the lounge for a while. ("Ah ha!" says my spouse, "I knew there was a Big Party!"). Yep, I'm gonna sit at the bar for a while with all the other guys ("Male bonding!', says my wife.) and we'll all stare at a basketball game on the Big Time Sports Network between NoName State and Ed's College of Auto Repair and Fashion Design. Yeah boy!

Hey, it's a good thing I love my job! See you in the bar…don't start the party without me! Okay?

FUN ALONG THE WAY

What's the recipe for success? I read somewhere that it's setting goals, effective planning, and hard work. Maybe that's so...On the other hand, perhaps it's just all about having fun.

I've known people who've sacrificed everything in pursuit of success–the long days, weekends, time with family and friends. They say, "If you want to be successful then you have to pay the price!". It seems to me that many have paid but too few have found success. Maybe they didn't pay enough?

Now here's the part that confuses me. Of the people I know who consider themselves successful (in whatever field they're in), I don't know many who believe they've paid a price for their success! In fact most of them tell me that the best part–the fun part—was getting there. Sure they worked hard but they found it to be incredibly enjoyable...and few would say they sacrificed family, friends, or the things that were important to them.

So here are a few of my alternative thoughts about success and fun...stop reading now if you don't want to hear workplace heresy.

- If it's not fun then you're not on the road to success–you're on the road to failure.
- If it's not fun, then do something else–immediately.
- Forget about the "big goals"–do what you love and the rest will take care of itself.
- Don't let anybody convince you it's not supposed to be fun (misery loves company).
- It takes courage to have fun...

And just in case you wondered, I'm having a great time!

WHY AREN'T YOU MOTIVATED?
(YOU THOUGHT YOU WERE!)

That's a terrible question to ask someone! I should know because I remember some years ago when Roger, my sales manager, asked me that very question! I also remember my answer. *"What do you mean? I'm motivated."* I felt angry, defensive, and maybe a little guilty...

"When I hired you, you were a ball of fire. I don't see it now. Your sales numbers are okay but they aren't what they once were", *he said.*

"What do you mean? I'm working hard. I've had a few bad breaks but I don't see why you're accusing me of not being motivated!"

"If you plan to keep working here, I better see some changes!"

The conversation went on for a good while and probably went from bad to worse. Roger thought I had a motivation problem and I thought Roger was wrong. He was the one with the problem! Roger's "negative motivation" worked for a while. At least I put on a good show of being "charged up". I started thinking about finding a better company to work for.

The passing of time let's you look back with painful clarity. Now I'll admit it. I had a motivation problem. The thing is, it just didn't feel like one at the time. I was working harder than ever; not slacking off. I wanted to make lots of money. Actually I *needed* to make lots of money with a first house and a first child! I wanted to be promoted. I wanted to be the top sales rep. So if I really wanted all these things so much, how could I possibly NOT be motivated???

I confused "wanting" and "effort" with "motivation". They're not the same. "Wanting" is focusing on the end success goal, but "Motivation" is the joy of making it happen. Confused? Try this example. A runner doesn't win the marathon because he or she wants victory the most. There are hundreds of people in the race who want to win just as much. A runner doesn't win because he or she trained the hardest or gave the greatest effort. There are hundreds of runners who trained harder or "gave it their all" and still didn't cross the finish line first. The Winner, however, loved every moment of the race itself. Excellence in the race was the real goal; the winning just the natural result.

And me? Well, I wanted to win but I forgot how to enjoy my job. I wasn't motivated.

Okay, you knew this question was coming. Take a deep breath…

"Are you motivated?"

Was today fun? Can you name three things that you did today that you know you did well and you feel fired up about? Did you make some progress on a deal, have a good idea, start something new? Did you feel some adrenaline today? Did you win (or even lose) today? Or was today just work?

If you're not satisfied with your answers, here's some good ways to get back on track!

Take another look at your Goals: What do you really want? More importantly WHY do you really want it? Promotion? Money? Recognition? Is it because *you* really want them or just because they're what everybody wants! Just thinking about what you *want and why* should set some of that adrenaline going. If not, maybe it's time to rethink. Think of your Goals as your power source that fuels your efforts.

Find the Friction: What's stopping you? Physics says that "an object in motion tends to stay in motion" unless it encounters friction or obstacles that slow it down. What's slowing you down? Identify your obstacles and then find some solutions, even if they're not perfect! Remember, if you can't find solutions you're destined to stop.

Set Your Path: Make your action plan. Focus on achieving your solutions. Write it down and live by your plan!

Take a Measure of Satisfaction: STOP! At the end of each day. Take some time to reflect on what you accomplished today–or even tried to accomplish. Celebrate a little!

Find Partnership: Like training for the marathon, running is more fun when you do it with someone. Being able to talk about and share the accomplishments (no matter how small) and even the disappointments of the day makes a big difference. Remember too that Success is never achieved alone.

Face Reality: Enjoy what you've done well, face honestly what you didn't do well. Being motivated isn't rose-colored glasses. Learn from successes as well as mistakes. You'll find even your mistakes motivate you!

The final Question: *"Did you enjoy today?"* Good, you're motivated!

COCKTAIL PARTY SHAME

Why would anyone actually want to be a salesman? Okay, so salesman isn't politically correct but this whole sales-person thing is so awkward. Actually I'm kind of in favor of Person-No-Specific-Gender-Charged-With-Selling-Responsibility or PNSGCWSR. Use of this clever, unpronounceable acronym with no vowel can issue in a new era of well-deserved respect and social status for those of us in the peddler profession.

For too long we in sales have endured "Cocktail Party Shame". As a party or other gathering proceeds we inevitably learn we are surrounded by corporate executives, nuclear physicists, educators, secret agents, physicians, cosmetologists, and the occasional astronaut. Each introduction is again invariably followed by a chorus of "My, what an interesting job! Tell me more!". There is one exception, of course. "Oh, you're in…sales? Really. How…uh, nice?" (Note: mentioning that without salespeople most other people wouldn't have a job is generally not an effective comeback at this point.)

We've all tried to disguise it, calling ourselves Account Executives, Marketing Representatives, or even Customer Consultants, but to no avail. Imagine however the potential prestige of proudly announcing, "Why Yes, I'm an PNSGCWSR!". Your inability to pronounce it of course only adds to your mystique and engenders fascination and admiration in all around you.

In recent totally unsubstantiated marketing tests of the PNSGCWSR concept, nine out of ten corporate executives said they would make time in their schedule to meet with a PNSGCWSR (although admitting they had never actually met one).

It works for me…

WHAT DO YOU WANT TO BE WHEN YOU GROW UP?

I remember in 4th Grade when the teacher went around the room asking "What do you want to be when you grow up". Kids said doctor, nurse, astronaut, jet pilot. The one's who watched too much TV said cowboy (or "cowgirl" whatever that is). I said "priest" (It was a Catholic school and you couldn't go wrong with priest.) But no one ever said "salesman". I mean, there were even some kids who said personal injury lawyer but not a single future salesman in the room! I wish I could find all those grown up kids today. I'd bet at least half of them are in sales!

Have you watched the sit-coms on TV? Can you think of even one where the lead character had anything to do with sales? Of course not; they all have neat jobs like doctors (ER), comedians (Seinfeld), architects (Mr. Brady), film makers (Mad About You), even HR directors (Drew Carey). Even the junk man (Sanford and Son) gets more play than a salesman!

Okay, so maybe selling isn't quite as exciting as the emergency room (but close!). Nonetheless I think it's time that Hollywood stopped ignoring us. We need movies and TV series that glorify being a salesperson. Personally I'm looking for something like Walker, Texas Salesman or maybe TOP (Sales)GUN.

I have a dream of an entire class of 4th Graders shouting out, in one voice, "We want to be Sales Reps!"

Nah, never happen!

PART II

ON SUCCESS...IN SELLING!

GOODBYE, BUFFALO BILL

The times of selling are changing. Are your salespeople the professionals they need to be to compete in today's market?

*   *   *   *   *

Traditional selling often reminds me of the Buffalo Hunters. In the old West, the buffalo hunters had a pretty good business going...for a while. They would sit up on a hill looking all around for herds of buffalo. When they found the herd, why then they would ride like hell after the generally unwilling buffalo, sharpshooting from horseback until they had killed all they could handle. It was a good business model...until the buffalo ran out.

The real successes in the Old West were *The Cattle Barons* who figured out that if you wanted to have a long term supply of livestock you had to "grow your own". So they fenced the land, tended and grew their herds, and built a limitless supply of "business" that they could simply herd in for "slaughter" as necessary.

We train most salespeople to be Buffalo Hunters. Traditional sales skills are often mostly sharpshooting skills, designed to "bring down" the unwilling prospect. The problem with selling this way is that with every new "hunting season" (quota year) there can be less and less "game" loose on the sales prairie. Salespeople need to become the new Cattle Barons—field marketers who know how to carefully plan, nurture, and grow the sales territory and who can develop long-term sources of business...that don't need a sharpshooter (who can hang upside down under a galloping horse) in order to make a close!

The only trouble is that becoming a cattle baron just isn't as exciting or as glamorous as being a buffalo hunter. There's not too much "thrill of the hunt". But times change. It's time for all you sales reps to hang up your buckskins, spurs, and buffalo rifles and wave "Goodbye, Buffalo Bill!".

GET HIRED BY YOUR CUSTOMER!

Okay, don't take this title too literally; the idea isn't to change jobs! I was just thinking that when a customer buys your product or service, he or she is really hiring you, your company, and your product to do a job that they need done.

Long ago (in a previous incarnation), I spent a number of years as a successful management "headhunter" and spent a lot of time coaching job candidates on how to "win" their interviews. I was looking back at an article I once wrote on interviewing skills and I realized that the same skills could be applied to sales calls with equal success. Here's just a few of my interviewing rules, applied today's salespeople:

1. **Interview for an Offer**–approach every sales call with one goal—to win! Sales decision cycles are much like the interview process. You keep interviewing up the ladder until you win or fall off.

2. **Be Enthusiastic**—more jobs—and more sales opportunities—are lost because the interviewee/salesperson tried to be too businesslike. Every company wants to hire or work with people who appear interested *in them* (not just themselves) and are personally "up".

3. **Smile**—okay, it sounds corny *but* your smile has an exceptionally powerful effect on your customer. I see a lot of sales reps and most smile very little if at all. The truth is that a sincere smile relaxes people and opens communication.

4. **Yes, No, & Maybe**—if anything is the secret to success in interviewing or selling, this may be it. These are the three possible answers to any customer question: "Yes I/we can!", "No, we can't/don't", and "Probably/Maybe". Would you hire someone who said or implied that "maybe I could do the job"? Would you buy from a salesperson who

said or implied that "maybe my product will meet your needs". Delete "maybe" and all its verbal cousins from your vocabulary!

Of course your customer could be so impressed with your "interviewing" sales skills that he or she makes you an offer you can't refuse. You never know...

POWERFUL PERSUASION?

Why are some salespeople better than others? Salespeople, managers, and sales training consultants have spent years trying to find the answer to that one. It really depends upon how you define the job of selling.

For example, I was taught that sales is the job of exerting "powerful persuasion". In other words, selling was a battle of sorts between me and the prospect. My task was to maneuver the prospect into a position from which he or she was absolutely unable to refuse my close! I did this through clever probing, using that information to present drop-dead features and benefits and to "overcome" any and all objections. Finally I called upon a series of direct and indirect "closing techniques" to bring home the deal. Nothing wrong with that since it seemed to work okay.

I call this kind of salesperson a "Call Specialist" and it is a job that frankly not everyone can do. The Call Specialist uses *sales techniques* plus *force of personality* to "move the prospect" to the desired outcome. That "force of personality"—a *killer instinct*—is by some considered to be the elusive selling success factor. Unfortunately it's hard to find and too often produces inconsistent and often unpredictable sales results.

I've found these days that there is another "type" of salesperson—one who is usually *more* successful and consistent but who doesn't appear to be a fast-talking *power persuader*—the "Solution Specialist". This salesperson asks the customer the same questions but uses them not to "manipulate" the prospect but as information tools to help jointly create a workable solution to a customer problem or desire. Instead of presenting product features and benefits, this salesperson "tries on" product solutions with the customer. *"What if we solved the problem this way? Have you considered…".* He or she closes powerfully as well but based on a "force of conviction", a personal belief in the solution reinforced by customer knowledge! Not too surprisingly, most customers actually like to buy from this salesperson.

To my mind, the elusive secret skills of selling don't have a lot to do with personality. I look for people who are fascinated by their customers, who enjoy finding creative solutions to problems, and who, when they think they've found a good solution, believe they're right—and are willing to say so!

SERIOUS RIDERS

I'm speaking tomorrow at a client's "Top Performers" conference. They were nice enough to invite me to come up a day early to join them during their "Recreation Day" at Whistler Resort in British Columbia. I'm no fool and I detect serious fun–so Canada here I come!

Besides the predictable golf outing, the recreation choices were mountain biking, backcountry ATV, horseback riding, and rock climbing. You can see that these are fun guys! I picked the ATV (all-terrain vehicle) trip up to the peak of Whistler mountain with six of the company's best sales reps. We bounced and careened through some mighty rough territory. Real "out on the edge" stuff. Now I'm sore, scratched, and soaking wet but what a great time! One of the best parts was when our guide, Dale, said he really enjoyed riding with a bunch of "serious riders"...of course that could have been due to the big tip. (No, I feel sure he meant it...he was very sincere.)

"Serious Riders". Sounds just like a bunch of top sales performers, doesn't it? To borrow a line from "The Eagles", they're the kind of people who always like to "take it to the limit...one more time". Top Performers want to maximize their business success and their entire lives, not just "do enough" or "make enough" to get by. They want *everything* that life can offer. Work or play, it's all the same.

Truth is, I don't really think you can be a top sales performer without this kind of attitude. What's more, I don't think you can be a "serious rider" at work without also being one in the rest of your life. It's not a learned skill, it's not genetically inherited, it's not a unique property of the chosen few, it's simply an *attitude*!...and anyone can have it if they want it.

I guess I'm the most surprised by people who don't try to "maximize" life for one reason or another. Why not? I suspect that some folks limit themselves by believing that success comes from hard work alone (and that they're not working hard enough), or that they don't deserve success, or that they lack the talent, or that they've had some bad breaks and haven't had the "luck" others have. It's another kind of *attitude*.

Bull poop! The thing is, you have to be successful in your own head before you can be successful in anything else. It's not a *result*, it's a *choice*—and when you make it, that's when you become a "Serious Rider"!

Well, enough said. I have to run—rock climbing starts in a half hour!

A MATTER OF TRUST

Not long ago I happened to be standing in the hallway in a large hotel conference center. I overheard a conversation between two sales executives during a break at their annual sales conference. One executive commented that the salespeople just were not responding to his attempts to motivate them.

"What's wrong with them? I've done everything I can think of!", he said.

The other executive thought for a moment and responded, "I think the problem is fear. They can't get motivated because they're not sure where we're going as a company and they're not sure what's going to happen to them!"

"Well we don't dare tell them about the merger," replied the first executive. "That would really get them worried!"

"I think you're underestimating them," said the second. "Let's try being up front with them and see what happens."

"Well, I don't know…"

In today's environment of acquisitions, mergers, corporate downsizing, and layoffs, people do have a lot to worry about. Many have lost the security that "doing a good job" brought in the past. The greatest "demotivator" of all is, in fact, *fear of the future.* That fear—and it's effect—is at its greatest when fueled by the unknown.

DON'T BE A TELESELLING WEENIE !

A reader called me this week, which is always a nice thing, with a question about telesales. Sometimes I'm amazed at just how big a part of selling telephone sales is today. What's more, I suspect it's about as difficult and frustrating as selling can get. This reader's question was simple, "Have you got any advice that can make me more successful?".

There must be a thousand books out there on telesales technique so I wondered what I could possibly say that was new. Something like "Here's a new, sure-fire idea that no one has thought of!". Well, I don't have any of those but I do have a lot of experience receiving telesales calls, so instead I gave this young sales rep a potential customer's perspective.

AT LEAST PRONOUNCE MY NAME RIGHT:

Nothing makes me end a telesales call faster than when you get my name wrong. For some reason, a lot of telesales reps pronounce "Mr. McMahon" something like "Mr. Mchamondd" or "Mr. Mac-Ma-Hone". *FYI, it's pronounced "Mac-Man".*

QUIT BEING SO DAMNED FRIENDLY!:

If you have a good offer for me, just tell me about it. I wish you could see my face (grimace, disgust) as you go through your litany of "So, how are you today, Mr. MacMahoney? How's the weather up there in New Hampshire?" I'm beginning to suspect that you're only interested in me and my climate so you can sell me something...

ENOUGH WITH THE CLEVER SALES TECHNIQUES!

This may be a shock, but trust me–there are no clever sales lines left that I (and every other telephone owner) haven't heard. Besides, none of them work and they irritate us. It reminds me of the adage, "Never try to teach a pig to talk. It won't work and it annoys the pig!"

SO WHAT DOES WORK?

Okay, here's the deal. If you get my name right, you've got a *maximum* of 5 to 8 *seconds* to sell me—not on buying but on listening more. That's your real sales call and should be your main objective! So you've only got time to do four things:

1. Introduce yourself and your company's name *(I'm Jane Doe from BigPhone International)*
2. Tell me what it is you're selling *(We provide worldwide long distance services…)*
3. Give me one, *specific killer* benefit *(Our typical residential customer saved $329.00 last year…)*
4. Ask me for more time *(Could I have just five minutes more of your time?)*

Sounds too simple to work, right? So who ever said sales had to be complex—except the guys who make up all that stuff!

So fifteen minutes later who calls me again? You got it…the same guy who just called for advice. But this time he's calling to sell ME and he's using the techniques I just gave him! I have to admit he's a quick learner.

So to prove myself right I end up buying $6,000.00 worth of vinyl siding…Swell!

PROFITABLE CUSTOMER RELATIONSHIPS

Sales representatives have traditionally been trained and goaled to do one thing: close sales. They are typically measured by gross sales attainment of quota objectives. However, just as management is changing, so is selling. Although fundamental sales skills will continue to be necessary and important, there is a new rule of selling:

Selling is not closing; selling is building Profitable Customer Relationships.

"Profitable Customer Relationships" may sound like a typical sales euphemism, a throw-away phrase, but in today's marketplace it is the critical factor of selling and understandable when we look at the component parts of this phrase.

"Customer Relationship"—The term "closing" suggests the "end" or completion of a deal or sales effort. In reality, each "close" should be a stepping stone to additional future business. Not only is future business the selling more of a product or service because the customer is satisfied with it, the future is in developing more business because the customer values the "professional relationship" he holds with the vendor. It is the relationship which not only drives more sales but which also serves to "competition-proof" the customer. Building such relationships requires the combination of sales or persuasive skills with unique customer knowledge— specifically an understanding of how we as a company contribute to the success of our customers and the managing of the customer's perception of real value.

"Profitable"—Providing "added-value" is the dominant sales trend today. Everyone is trying to do it. The problem is that it can put a company out of business unless managed correctly—and one large corporation

29

almost achieved this. Corporation X developed an aggressive added-value program for its customers to offer them greater services than the competition and unique sources of product and industry expertise. As with any value-added effort there was a cost in doing this that reduced sales margins; however, corporate planned to offset this through being able to justify fewer discounts, customer retention, and increased business. Unfortunately, the salespeople conducted business as usual—they delivered the added-value as instructed but also continued to cut price when faced with a competitor's lower bid, cutting margins even further. Why did they do it and why did sales management allow it?…because the goals were ultimately still the same: gross sales dollar revenue.

Building "Profitable Customer Relationships" requires a re-engineering of the entire sales process, the role of the salesperson, how salespeople are goaled and measured, and especially how they are managed. The role of a sales manager expands again—not only coach and resource but also investment manager, responsible for assuring a solid return on investment from the sales program.

TICKETS OR ENTERTAINMENT?

I sat on a plane not long ago and found myself speaking to a passenger who happened to own a movie theater. He told me that ticket sales were really up of late and that was good news for him and his business. Ticket-sales? Hmmm…

"It's interesting that you say 'ticket' sales", I said, "since that's not really what you sell."

He gave me a funny look and our conversation came to a rather abrupt end. He probably thought I was a little nuts to say something like that.

About 15 minutes later he looked over at me and said "You're right. I don't sell tickets. I sell entertainment. Tickets are just how I keep score!". We talked for some time and decided that what he really sold was laughter, tears, dreams, and even some education. Tickets were his "product" (that thing that he "sold"), but people only bought his tickets because they wanted something else.

Isn't this true with almost every product? Are your buying because they want the physical product you sell or because they really want what it will do for them.

My new friend's final comment was, "You know, if I just sold tickets, I'd be out of business. Not a lot of people collect tickets."

Are you selling tickets or entertainment?

SELLING AT THE TOP

It starts with "Asking the Question":

One day I asked a customer, "What can we do to help you better achieve your goals?". He didn't really have an answer for me other than "Keep doing what you're doing"; but he said he was surprised that I asked the question.

"Why?", I asked.

"Well, most salespeople just want to make the sale and aren't too interested in much else."

"I want the same thing," I answered. "I also want to make the next sale and the next sale. That's only going to happen if your company is doing well, so it's in my interests to ask that question."

The truth is that I never got a more detailed answer to my question but I get their business more often than not–and just because I asked that question.

Traditional sales logic says "Sell at the Top"; in other words, sell as high in the organization as possible. It's a good strategy but as most professional salespeople know, it's a lot easier said than done! You're right when you say that your customer's execs don't want to see you. There's two reasons:

1. They hire people to make product decisions. The Execs are worried about running the business, not buying an office product.

2. They don't think you have anything to talk about that would be of real interest to them either.

Think of your customer's organization as having two levels–Executive and Operations. At the operations level you are dealing with buyers who have very tactical needs. They are evaluating products based on specifications, price, and suitability to meet a defined operational need. Chances are that you do a pretty good job already of selling to these folks.

At the Executive level, they're worrying about business issues–large-scale business development strategies, effective cost and resource management, and achieving high return-on-investment. The Executive level differentiates vendor relationships–some are Strategic Partners and some are Commodity Suppliers. A strategic partner brings something more to the table (value)–a win/win strategy for mutual business success that is usually based upon the supplier's expertise or resources–and is always more than the supplier's product!

To sell at the Top, you and your company will have to:

1. Craft a value proposition that will position you as a strategic partner.

2. You will have to gain a clear understanding of your customer's business goals, current issues, and planned business direction and initiatives. That's a lot more than just knowing their needs!

3. Develop business scenarios; e.g., "We understand you face the following issues. Working together we know that we can help you address them!"

4. Sell Direct to the Top–generally speaking, your contacts at the Operations level are rarely going to get you executive access. They're likely not too interested in your goal to be a strategic partner with the company and may not be enthusiastic about you "bothering" the executives. There's no easy solution–if you want to sell at the top you're going to have to go after it on your own.

5. A Different Product–when you're selling at the exec level, remember that your product is no longer your product. The execs are not interested in buying your office equipment so don't try to sell something the customer doesn't care about. Your new product is the value you and your company bring to the table and this is what you have to SELL. The purchase of your physical product is a happy by-product of making the Value Sale.

WHERE PRICE IS NOT AN ISSUE

Do your customers demand lower prices? Do you find yourself negotiating price with every deal? Would it surprise you that there are salespeople who almost never negotiate and almost always get their asking price? Who never lose a deal over price? And they're selling today to YOUR customers!

Have you been to your doctor recently...your tax accountant or CPA...maybe your lawyer? Did you negotiate for a lower price? Probably not. If my doctor or CPA had negotiable pricing I might be a little suspect about his or her real abilities. It's generally accepted, in fact, that the best are always the most expensive. That's they way it is with professionals.

Your customers go to the doctor or lawyer or accountant too. They just call them consulting firms or corporate counsel. These professionals most always get their asking price–and the better they're known or the more expert their staffs the more they charge. Your customers pay it because they know "you get what you pay for". And by the way, the consultants and lawyers and financial people they buy from are salespeople just like you (even though they might shudder at the thought...).

So what's the difference between you and them? It's the customer's perception!

Customers tend to believe that "The Professionals" are as interested in helping the client (customer) as in making money for themselves. Don't you believe that your doctor is more interested in curing your illness than the fee...or that your tax specialist is most interested in helping you minimize your taxes?

You and your company may bring every bit as much expertise and value to the table as any consulting firm–value that's worth paying for! Unfortunately many customers feel that their "Suppliers" are less interested in their customers and more interested in how much they can sell. They believe that the price you ask for your product does not reflect the value you bring, that it's always too high, and that you even expect it to be negotiated downward.

If you want to be viewed as one of "The Professionals" you have to learn to do what they do—sell more than the quality of your product; sell what it and you can really DO for your customer!

IF THEY DON'T KNOW ABOUT YOU

Years ago I learned what I believe is the basic rule for sales success. Here it is: **If they don't know about you, they can't buy from you!**

No matter how good your product or service is ñ or how good your face-to-face selling skills are ñ it doesn't matter if no one knows about you. It's called marketing!

Something else I learned as well: if they know the right things about you then the selling part gets really easy.

The truth is, I never really liked that "selling" thing. You know, me vs. the unwilling prospect who finally falls to the overwhelming power of my sales techniques. Too much work and stress. I like it better when prospects come to me. So I learned to become a marketer" as well as a "salesman". I started looking for simple, creative ways to get my message out to as many prospects and customers as possible; to drive enthusiastic prospects to my door. Today I follow my 80/20 rule: 80% marketing time, 20% selling time.

As I travel around, I find that many salespeople think that marketing and sales are separate, that it's the job of the company to create new leads (marketing) and the job of salespeople to close them (selling). What a perfect world that would be! Truth is that every salesperson needs to learn to do both jobs—market and sell in your own territory.

Don't rely on someone else to do the 80% for you. If they don't know about you, they can't buy from you. If they know about you, they'll come and buy from you.

THE PEEPING TOM SYNDROME

Are you a salesperson afflicted with the dreaded "Peeping Tom Syndrome"? Old Peeping Tom looked in windows and no one ever knew he was there. Sometimes selling can be the same.

Our ability to provide real value to our customers–and gain the competitive advantage that results from it -fireally comes down to our knowledge of the customer. It's what we know about the customer's business needs, issues, goals, and plans that allows us to become an added-value partner in his success. It's what we know that enables us to develop the sales strategies and tactics to build and maintain this powerful, competition-proof relationship.

Does your customer know and really appreciate just how much you understand about his or her business? About his needs, issues and goals? Does he or she know that you actively work to use this knowledge to better serve him? That you have an active interest in his business success? Or does he think that all you know is your own product and company; and that your prime objective is only to move product?

Unlike Peeping Tom, when we look in the customer's window it's important that he knows we're there!

PART III

ON VALUE SELLING!

THE VALUE PRINCIPLE

Transcript from a recent executive meeting at NoName Corporation:

Charles Smith, CEO of NoName : Ladies and gentlemen, our competition is increasing. They have just significantly lowered their prices and our customers are pressuring us to do the same. The problem is, I really don't want to cut prices. I feel it's a poor competitive strategy but it may be our only option. Before I go ahead with a cut I want to hear your thoughts..

Ann Baxter, Support Services Director: Well, I think it's clear. We provide the best service and support in the industry. Our customers should be reminded how important that is to them. We shouldn't have to sell at a lower price!

Terry Sheldon, Sales & Marketing Director: Ann, I agree we have the best service but our competitor's is pretty good too. It's just not enough to counter the price difference. If we're not going to lower prices then we need new products!

Carl Martin, Manufacturing Manger: Terry, we just don't have any new products in the pipeline for this year. The good news, however, is that with the additional manufacturing capacity we put in, we've been able to fill 99% of all customer orders on-time. Our quality is the best in the industry! Shouldn't these be important to our customers?

Terry: It should be, Carl. In sales, our people have worked hard to build stronger relationships with our customers! We've done customer focus groups and surveys, needs analysis, and even joint business planning with our key accounts. Still, I don't know if it's enough.

Anita Carson, IT Director: In IT we've implemented new systems for Customer Relationship Management, Supply Chain, Data Warehousing, and a new Internet site. All of these make it easier for our customers to work with us. I would think that should have some value to our customers!

Charles: You all make some very good points. You've all worked hard developing customer value programs. But to tell you the truth when it comes to price, I'm just not really sure that our customers care all that much about our value programs. No, I think what we'll do is go ahead and cut our prices to match our competitor's. I want manufacturing to try and get some kind of new product out in three months. I want salespeople to start making more calls. We're all going to have to tighten our belts ñ we'll start by reducing expenses and canceling the new hires we planned. We may have to make some personnel cuts, and...

* * * * *

It sounds good. Like our hypothetical NoName Corporation, we would like our customers to buy from us because of the "Total Value Package" (TVP) we offer them: quality products, excellent service and systems, our ability to meet their needs and requirements, and the strong relationships built by our sales organization–all provided at a fair price that represents a good value to the customer and a honest profit to us. Our Total Value Package should be our greatest source of Competitive Advantage! It ought to work that way but it often doesn't.

Product and Price keep getting in the way. Despite our best efforts, it seems that when a competitor lowers prices or introduces a new product, the value of all our added-value goes right out the window! It shouldn't but it, again, too often does.

We're tempted to say, "The customers really don't care about added-value!", but somehow that doesn't seem quite right. We innately know that they should care. Are they aware of our TVP (we've probably spent a lot of sales and marketing time telling them about it)? Maybe they don't care enough? If they don't know, don't care, or don't care enough, we have to ask WHY?. What are we doing wrong?

The problem is in how we "sell" Value. Actually we "tell" value more than sell it! We often do an excellent job of telling our customers about all the unique value we offer them. We tell them, hopefully, how this Value benefits them. We tell them why it should be a deciding factor in their purchase decisions. The customers nod their heads, appear to agree with us, and we think we've sold them on our Value package ñ locked out the competition, won the day, and created loyal customers. And that lasts just until "product" and "price" rear their ugly heads once again!

THE VALUE PRINCIPLE

The answer lies in the **First Concept of The Value Principle:**

Value is created in the mind of the customer when it is transformed from something we PERCEIVE to something the Customer EXPERI-ENCES!

We know the Value that we offer the customer. We know why the customer should appreciate it. We know why the customer should base their buying decision on it. And perhaps we have done a pretty fair job of telling the customer about it. Our customers hear us; they say they understand and agree with what we're saying. We all perceive the same thing. But all the perceived value in the world doesn't matter unless the customer clearly experiences our value!

In other words, when a customer does not value the Total Value Package we provide them, it's not necessarily because they don't know about it; it's because they haven't really experienced it.

What does it mean for a customer to "experience" value?

The **Second Concept of The Value Principle** states:

"Successful Customers Buy More !"

The best customers are those whose businesses are successful. If they are successful then they are in a position to continue to purchase from us and may likely even increase their purchase volumes. The converse is obvious: Unsuccessful customers will buy less. As providers or products or services it is clearly in our best interests to help our customers' businesses become more successful. Ultimately, this should be the bottom-line purpose of all the Value we are trying to provide our customers: to help make them more successful.

We can say, then, that a customer will experience our Value when he or she achieves increased business success as a direct result.

The challenge this concept presents to our sales, marketing, and service organizations is to do more than just sell value–that's just the starting point. The real task is to assure that the customer's company actually achieves the maximum potential of our Value. Our ability to make our customers more successful then becomes our true source of Competitive Advantage in the marketplace. It is also the leverage that allows us to successfully command a premium price for our products and services.

Still unanswered is the question, "How do we then 'transform' our Total Value Package into customer business success?" and leads us to The **Third Concept of The Value Principle:**

"To transform 'Perceived Value' into 'Experienced Value', our Expertise in the Business of our Customers Must be as Great as our Expertise in our Own Business."

Clearly we cannot expect to know all aspects of our customer's businesses as well as they do, but we can build the kind of relationships that will enable us to understand their challenges and business issues as well as their current and planned business strategies and initiatives. We can qualify and quantify how our Total Value Package can positively impact each of these!

To accomplish this, however, may require a real change in how many of our own people do their jobs. For example, a salesperson is typically viewed as an expert in presenting his or her company and it's products and services. A salesperson's job has been to show a customer how a product or service meets a stated customer need or requirement. It has traditionally been left up to the customer to translate meeting a need or requirement into increased business success.

A Value Principle salesperson (and Company) would have a depth of customer knowledge and an understanding of business issues that would allow him or her to work with a customer at both a technical or product level and at a business level, actively helping the customer transform the TVP into increased business success, i.e. Experienced Value. This means that a salesperson must be capable of having executive-level conversations with customers, not just product-level ñ for many a very new skill set.

When, as an organization, a company gains this level of customer knowledge and expertise, it also gains the ability to develop and target its total package of value and significantly enhances its ability to truly leverage Value for competitive advantage.

VALUE AND SUCCESS

I've said it over and over. Creating Value is about creating Success for our customers! It's perhaps the one great truth–everyone is working hard to be successful! I didn't always believe that, and you may not either. How many people–customers, co-workers, or friends–have you known who didn't seem to want to be successful. Did you ever say something like "he/she just doesn't seem motivated" or "he/she just isn't willing to make the effort"? Do you know people who don't appear to be successful and don't seem to be doing anything about it? Sure, we all know these folks.

The problem isn't that they don't want to be successful; it's that we're viewing them through our eyes and how we view success. As salespeople we tend to equate success with accomplishment and personal growth. We are focused on winning because that's the nature of what we do. We want life to get better. We climb mountains as a matter of course every single day.

Believe it or not, there are people who have absolutely no desire for our kind of success. They want their own kind. "Okay," you ask, "what DO they want?

For some Success is achieving security and safety, limiting risk and uncertainty, and maintaining what they have. Like in the story of the tortoise and the hare, the turtle says that "slow and steady" is the way to win.

For some Success is found in their relationships, not what they accomplish. They want to live and work with people they like and who like them. They want to feel they're part of something. They want to trust and be trusted. Family may be their greatest success and the time they have to spend with them.

Some may see Success as an opportunity to be creative, or to gain recognition for their ideas, to become a bigger fish in their own pond, or to be noticed and valued by others.

And some are just like us…

If Value is created when we create success for our customers then we have to ask ourselves how each customer defines his or her Success before we can create a powerful Value Proposition!

CUSTOMER APPRECIATION DAYS

Everybody's busy "appreciating" their customers these days. It's good business to let customers know how much we value their business. As a customer myself, I know I like to feel appreciated with a few nice words from my sales rep. Golf outings are real nice too! Some of my vendors appreciate me so much that I'm planning on asking them for a bigger discount next time I buy. I'm sure they'll give it to me because keeping my business is clearly so important to them! I like this customer appreciation stuff…

It occurred to me the other day that we're missing something here. It's true that we want to let our customers know how much we appreciate them. The real goal, however, ought to be *making sure our customers appreciate US!*

Think of it this way: the products and services that we sell bring *value* to our customers; that is, we help them meet or fulfill a need that they have. To accomplish that, we as sellers make significant investments in time, personnel, R&D, service, marketing, and the like and we then attempt to sell at a fair price. Most customers, however, remain blissfully unaware of how hard we're actually working to assure their satisfaction! There's two ways to keep customers:

- The first is by letting them know how much we love them.
- The second is making sure they understand just how hard we are working for them.

It's a matter of sales leverage as well—the customer who appreciates *us* is not only more loyal but also far less price sensitive than one who just feels appreciated!

It's a whole new slant on "Customer Appreciation Day"!

THE POWER OF CUSTOMER KNOWLEDGE

There is no more powerful selling tool than customer knowledge. In fact, it is the key to Value Selling. The question is not whether you know your customers. It's whether you could know more!

If you're like most people, you just answered "I know my customers pretty well. No problem there!"…and now you're going to quit reading this article. But hold on for just a minute, okay?

Recently I worked with a client who was developing a national account plan for a major financial conglomerate. The plan required the account manager to collect detailed information about how the customer did business, their organizational and decision structures, the business obstacles faced by the customer and their initiatives for growth, and much more.

I don't know how much it did for that sales rep but it did a lot for me. A few weeks later I happened to be sitting on an airplane next to an executive of that same financial conglomerate. After a while we found ourselves talking about his company and how business was going in today's economy.

"Did you used to work for us or are we a client of yours? You seem to know everything about us", he asked.

In fact, he was so impressed with my depth of "customer knowledge" that they're now becoming a client. In short, he perceives that I bring two things to the table that are "Valuable" to his company:

(1) My product–the skills I have, and…

(2) My Knowledge–the ability to apply my product to his company's specific needs to achieve maximum results.

Customer Knowledge IS the root of Value…and the Power of Selling!

VALUE VS. COMMODITY

Some thoughts for the new year rattling around in my head…

Why do people buy? I suppose there could be two reasons…because they want to or because they don't want to.

Hold on! People buy when they don't want to?

Sometimes people buy because they're put in a position where it's hard to say "No". (A lot of sales training technique is devoted to this kind of selling. It might work fine if you only plan to make one sale to each customer.)

Sometimes they buy because they have to have something, even if they really don't want it very much–or perhaps they have no real supplier or product choices. It's called "Commodity Selling".

Personally I would rather sell to people who actually want to buy something.

The reason people want to buy is that they perceive Value to themselves. In other words, they believe that purchasing a product or service will help them achieve something they want—meet a goal, resolve a problem, become more successful, etc. If everything works out, then you have a happy customer who will buy again and again.

Selling Value doesn't take a lot of technique but it does take a lot of curiosity. Salespeople who effectively sell Value are more interested in their customer's business than their own. They ask a lot of questions–not to develop "traps" but to better understand how best to serve the customer.

Frankly, it's a lot more work to sell Value than to just make Commodity sales calls, but consider this:

People who buy commodities want to buy as little as possible for the lowest possible price.

People who buy Value-producing products want to buy as much as they can and expect to pay a premium.

Is your product a Commodity item (or viewed as such by customers)? Make it a Value Product by understanding and measuring how your product contributes to your customer's success.

VALUE: SUCH A FRAGILE THING!

What a fragile thing customer Value is. It takes so much effort to create and so little effort to destroy.

A major airline spends thousands of dollars to tell me how important I am to them. They send me bundles of first-class upgrades, special "money-saving" offers, and they even let me board first. Their advertising tells me how enjoyable they're trying to make my business flying experience. I've believed them and flown with them whenever I could...until one day my airplane suffers a malfunction and my flight is cancelled. I've *got* to be in my destination city that evening and so I'm looking for a little of that extra special service. Then I run into a ticket agent with an "attitude".(If you fly a lot you know exactly what I mean!) Suddenly I'm ready to start taking my business to another airline.

My credit card company showers me with Value as well. They offer me a host of worldwide services, discounts on rental cars and hotels, and double the manufacturer's warranty on major purchases when I use their card. At Christmas they even sent me "free" thank-you-for-your-business gifts (although I had to pay the postage—which didn't make a lot of sense). But then there was the month that I was just a tad late paying my bill. I didn't mind the telephone call and I fully agreed that they have the right to expect to be paid on time. What I did mind was the warning I received from their customer "service" representative who pointedly said that *this better not happen again!* I've decided I don't really like these people and I don't want to use their credit card.

I stopped at my favorite restaurant this morning for a cup of coffee and a muffin before a long automobile ride to a client. It's a restaurant chain that spends a lot of money advertising their friendly stores and smiling people. I handed the waitress a $20 bill and she *grunted*, "Don't you have anything smaller?" "No", I said, "that's the way it came out of the ATM this morning." She could have smiled; instead I get the big sigh and the look of disgust. Tomorrow I'll go to a different shop.

I will admit my attitude is possibly a tad immature. After all, how can I blame an entire airline, a credit card company, or a restaurant chain just because one of its employees didn't measure up to my high expectations? Shouldn't I be understanding that sometimes everyone has a bad day? In my heart I know I should be…but I'm not.

I am beginning to suspect that just because a company's advertising says that that they are "helpful and friendly" it isn't necessarily true. It's just good advertising copy. I suspect that when a company says it "really wants my business" that doesn't mean it really cares about my satisfaction. It's just a good sales pitch. I suspect that too many companies are thinking more about how to "get" my business and not much time planning how to "keep" it.

Perhaps this wouldn't be a problem if I'm the only one who felt this way; but sadly I suspect I'm not. Despite the advertising and the sales pitches and the "Value" programs, too many customers don't believe that many vendors or suppliers want anything more than their money *today*. By the same token, many companies seem to think that the quality of their products and all the Value services they offer should make up for an "occasional" lapse in customer relations or service.

Many companies offer "Value" but what we need are more "Value companies". Anyone can offer what they call Value products and services. It is a very special company, however, that sees its primary mission as creating successful, satisfied, and loyal customers–and recognizes that *this* is its principal product, not the physical products it sells.

The *Value Company* is an organisation based on leadership and a common vision, one shared by *every* employee. It is more than the corporate mission statement (another piece of advertising copy) but it does begin at the top. Many of the greatest companies of the 20th century can trace their success to the Value vision of their founders and leaders. For example Thomas J. Watson of IBM founded and infused a worldwide organisation with his vision that IBM's success would be found in the success of its customers. Most importantly, IBM's customers knew this and it was a rare employee of IBM who didn't put the customer first.

As businesspeople, it is time that we think less about how to create Value by giving our customers more and more. It's time instead that we think about how to create sales and service organisations based on a *Value vision*. After all, added value is such a fragile thing…

SELLING THE FUTURE

I just bought life insurance last evening, a ton of it. My wife is awfully happy these days…after all she'll be a rich woman someday. Until that day comes I get to pay for what the insurance guys call "peace of mind". I can't tell you how "peaceful" it makes me feel to know that "the good life" starts immediately following mine. Oh well…

As we left the insurance agent my wife said, "Why don't we go out for a drink to celebrate!". Celebrate? Other than that wonderful "peace of mind" which is costing me an arm and a leg, contemplating my eventual demise didn't put me in a real celebrating mood. Now if they sold insurance that can insure that I *keep* living, but…) So I went back to see my insurance agent, who did feel like celebrating!.

"Jim", I said, "since I'm paying for all this insurance and, as far as I can tell, get none of the material benefits, don't you think you could give me a little 'closing gift' or something? Maybe a set of Cross pens? You know, just so I could go out with Sue and feel like I got something for my purchase too?"

Jim thinks I'm crazy, and reminds me again of all the "peace of mind" I now have. Why don't I feel better?

Actually this experience taught me something important about selling "Value". See, I don't believe that anyone actually *wants* to buy life insurance. What we do want to buy is *the Future*.

If you think about it, *every single product* you buy is not purchased for what it *is*. It's bought for what you believe it will do for you in the future, i.e. after you buy it.

For example, we buy food in anticipation of the enjoyment of eating it…or a performance automobile for the fun of driving it. We buy business product and services in the belief that they will help us become more successful, make our lives easier, or avoid future problems.

It seems to me that it's time we quit selling products and started selling the real future those products represent for our customers!

PRODUCTS OR CONSEQUENCES

When I was a kid every breakfast cereal had free stuff "inside this box!". (They don't do that anymore; nowadays you have to *send in* for them.) Since most cereals tasted pretty good and I didn't much care which one I ate for breakfast, I always picked the one with the most or the best freebies. Last week I bought some new software. There were several packages that appeared pretty much equal but one came with *bonus free software*! Guess which one I bought? Little boys never really grow up...

Is that what Value is all about? Added *freebies*? Obviously I can't say that it doesn't work, but there seems to be something inherently wrong when people buy products based less on the products themselves and more on the freebies. In other words, is the only way a company can differentiate itself from the competition by finding things to give away–add-ons, services, and of course the product itself (discount pricing)?

We perhaps know what *selling* is all about, but we have forgotten what *buying* is all about!

People do not buy *Products*! People buy *Consequences*. They buy what they believe will be the *result* of purchasing a product. Folks don't buy houses, they buy homes; they don't buy insurance, they buy safety; they don't buy "precision-engineering", they buy "no problems". In other words, *I buy the product or service that I believe will result in the best consequences!* The best consequences are the real Value...

So ask yourself this question: "What are we selling these days...products or consequences?". Let's keep the freebies in the cereal boxes where they belong.

PAPERBACK RIDER

Once in a while I come across a real example of Value. This story might sound like a little thing but after I tell you I think you'll agree with me that it's unique—and we'll give some credit to a good company...

Not long ago I flew from Boston to Seattle on Delta Air Lines. It's a long flight, so after my laptop computer battery gave up the ghost I switched to reading a less-than-exciting paperback novel I picked up in the airport. I finished the book just before we landed, put it in the seat pocket in front of me, and promptly forgot about it. Later I figured that I had made a donation to the flight attendant's library. Sound familiar?

I met with my client the next two days and returned to the airport on Friday for my trip home. Waiting in the gate area for the flight to board I heard the page, "Would Timothy McMahon please check in with the gate agent?". I'm thinking there's some problem with my upgrade, they've given away my seat, or some other God-awful thing that can only happen on a Friday when you're trying to get home. But you know what's coming, don't you?

"Mr. McMahon, you left this book on Wednesday's flight. We thought you might want it."

Actually it was a really bad novel and I really didn't want it; but of course I wasn't going to tell her that. Instead I thought about how much effort someone at Delta had to take to save that book, look up my return flight, and have it waiting for me at the gate—and all for a cheap paperback! It would have been so much easier just to trash it with no one the wiser.

The point is that right now I really like Delta Air Lines! Why? Because someone at Delta actually cared about ME. It wasn't about customer satisfaction—the flight was fine. Instead someone treated me the way they would have liked to be treated—and created Value in the process. Imagine what would happen if everyone took that attitude!

Your customers know you care about their business but do they think you care about them? Would you make the extra effort?

DO YOUR CUSTOMERS NEED YOUR SALESPEOPLE?

We all know why companies need salespeople but have you ever asked yourself whether your customers need your salespeople? While it's true that "people buy from people they like" it's even truer that people buy from people they "need".

The traditional tasks of a salesperson are:

1. To explain the features of a product that the customer isn't familiar with.

2. To act as the vendor's representative in negotiating price or other terms

3. To "service" the account—assure satisfaction and address any problems that come up pre- and post-sale.

4. To build a "personal relationship" with the customer

These are all well and good but may not add up to a lot in the mind of the customer.

So why would a customer or prospect need a salesperson?

1. To help them solve an identified business problem or avoid future ones.

2. To suggest ways to improve the customer's business using the salesperson's products or services (based on having an in-depth knowledge of the business).

3. To be a reliable source of needed information and expertise.

4. To assure product performance.

The two words that come to mind are ADVISOR and RESOURCE. To put it another way, do your customer's see your salespeople as members of their "success team"? If they do then you've got real competitive advantage!

THE SALES MOUSETRAP

How do you sell? What's your sales approach…your selling advantage? Is it product?…or price?…or service. The answers—and Mousetrap Theory—may have more of an effect on your future in selling than you imagine.

What is "Mousetrap Theory"? In the late 19th century, the poet Ralph Waldo Emerson said, "Build a better mousetrap and the world will beat a path to your door! "Ralph was a great poet; but no one, as far as I can determine, ever remembered him as a master salesman—and probably for good reason. Mousetrap theory just plain doesn't work.

The proof of "mousetrap's failure can be seen in the scattered remains of the hundreds of high-tech start-up companies opened in the late 70's and early 80's. Often they were started by exceptional engineers with ideas for a whole new generation of better mousetraps—except that they were called microchips or networks or software.

They produced detailed "spec sheets" for their hot new products, sent out technical press releases, demonstrated at trade shows, and waited for the orders to roll in…and waited…and waited. Finally, many hired a sales-manager-slash-sales-representative if it wasn't too late and the money wasn't running out. Usually it was and it did; and the engineers, still scratching their heads, closed up shop and returned to the big corporations, still not completely sure what went wrong.

There are a lot of mousetrap salespeople in the marketplace today. They don't necessarily sit and wait for the orders to come in but they do rely on their product to do the real selling for them. Sadly, like all those ill-fated start-ups, they're probably doomed as well—it's maybe just not quite that obvious yet

VALUE IN A DOWN ECONOMY

Every professional sales rep and manager knows that there are good times and there are bad times. The economy is cyclic, that is, good times don't last forever (and, Thank God, neither do bad ones!). Let's take a minute and think about what doing business in a "down" economy really means. Since we've had so many good economic years, there are a lot of salespeople out there who have never been through a recession or a downturn. So here's a few thoughts worth remembering…for them and all of us.

1. Even in a down economy, some businesses (and salespeople) do grow and prosper. They aggressively choose to find and win every piece of profitable available business.

2. A recession means that there is simply not enough business to go around. Not every supplier in a market is going to make his or her goals.

3. If you want business, you're going to have to take it away from someone else. If you can do that successfully and consistently then you will be the one who grows and prospers.

4. In a down economy you and your company simply can't afford to take unprofitable business. When you do you are doing yourself, your company, and your customers a disservice.

5. Your greatest sales and marketing tool is the success of your company. Companies want to buy from growing, successful vendors because they know you will continue to be there for them.

6. Your customers want to grow and prosper today as much as you do. They need to hear win/win propositions from you. Pick the companies in your marketplace who are going to be successful, win their business, and hitch your star to their growth.

7. To be successful you're really, absolutely, positively going to have to SELL. You'll need to flawlessly execute every skill you have (and maybe a few you're going to have to learn), use every bit of knowledge you can find on your customers and their needs, and polish every technique until they glow!

You know that there are changes…big changes…out there in the world of selling. Some are obvious and some perhaps not quite so obvious.

The obvious ones are simple–a down economy, corporate cutbacks and "right-sizing", budget constraints, and the like. The "not-so-obvious" ones, however, come down to these two statements:

1. In the past, a sales rep had to convince the customers why they should select his or her product over the competition. Today, the successful sales rep has to first convince the customer just to BUY…and THEN to select his/her product.

2. Customers are trying to cut costs. They're aggressively looking for lower prices from their vendors. They're "right-sizing" (downsizing) their purchases. The successful sales reps will show their customers new ways to create ROI (return on investment); that is, how to achieve greater business results by buying more product, not less!

Traditionally the solution in a down economy was to exhort salespeople to sell harder, make more calls, and unfortunately to cut prices to the bone when necessary. But remember that ultimately, our success is a reflection of the success of our customers. Activity and hard selling are not going to make a customer buy more or pay a premium price for our products. Ultimately our sales success will depend upon salespeople's ability to deliver a powerful "value proposition"–a true "success proposition"–that creates a more successful customer!

MORE TALES FROM THE ROAD...EXPERIENCING VALUE?

My wife doesn't like me to talk to salespeople. Specifically she doesn't like me to be part of any purchase that involves us with a salesperson. I suppose it's because I get incredibly irritated by bad sales reps and feel this urge to point it out during the call. Cruel? Possibly but I can't help myself...

I really tried to restrain myself yesterday...

I saw an ad in the Boston Globe for one of the major cell phone providers. It looked like they had a pretty good deal and the ad said that they were focused on meeting the real needs of business users. Guys like me–that's good. Reading the ad, they've got a pretty powerful Value Proposition! So I figured it's worth a call. The ad, of course, still left me with a few questions about the different rate plans, international access, and such. If everything was as stated I was ready to cancel my current provider and become their customer right then and there! So I called...

The list of irritations and real stupidity is just too long to relate but it begins with a perky "customer service representative" who I can't understand, who has to ask for my name and address three times because (supposedly) his computer keeps going down, who tells me he has never heard of New Hampshire and is that a state?, and says that his computer will not accept New Hampshire. This confusion is of course because we learn he spells it "Nuhamshere". But I am patient...

A half hour has gone by and I point out (nicely I think) that although I understand they want to collect information on me, I just have a few key questions so I can make a decision NOW. He tells me he just needs one more thing and all my questions will be answered. It seems his computer has indicated that my email address is invalid. But I AM patient...

After spelling the email SIX TIMES, it's Showtime! "Okay," I say, "here's what I need to know."

"One moment please, sir", he says, "I will now connect you to a business specialist who will answer all your questions. Please hold." (Click)

"Thank you for calling XXXXXX", says the recorded voice. "We are experiencing high caller volume and you will be connected to the next available salesperson. Approximate wait time is…21 minutes. Thank you for your patience and we appreciate your business". Okay, since they said they appreciate me I'll wait. And I am patient…

And finally she comes on! A real salesperson. Someone who will care! After all we're both salespeople. But clearly I shouldn't have called late in the day because she's tired and maybe just a little bit cranky. Abrupt is too kind a word. Rude comes to mind. And guess what? They're having computer problems and the information the service rep collected was deleted. "So could I have you name again, sir?"

"Hold on", I said. "Your ad says you specialize in meeting the needs of business people and you're in business to help me do more business. Is that true? Then why have you wasted an hour of my precious business time collecting pointless data when you might have been helping me solve a business problem? You call this 'selling'?" . And that's when she hung up (probably another computer malfunction).

The point? One of "The Value Principles" is that "Value must be transformed from something the customer initially perceives into something the customer experiences!" I "perceived" their value proposition from their ad, but like so many ads, it was only words. What I "experienced" was something very different.

PART IV

SOME OLD YANKEE WISDOMS 'N
SUCH!

ON OLD YANKEES, SLED DOGS, AND THE BUSINESS OF WINNING

Up here in my home state of New Hampshire there's more than a few "old yankees" around and there's still a bit of "old yankee wisdom" floating about—some that I've found has some real value for salespeople.

Down the road lives my neighbor, Oren, a pretty authentic old yankee as they go. No one is really sure just how old Oren is, but he's definitely seen more than a few New England winters. Now if you were to ask Oren how deep the snow was last year, he'd most likely tell you it was about "chest high on a duck, (ayuh)." Ask him how far someplace is and it's usually about "from heah to theah". There's a lot of yankee wisdom I haven't figured out yet...

Not long ago Oren asked me just what it was that I do for a living. I explained that for years I had been a salesrep and managed sales and now I write books and speak to companies and organizations on selling and managing.

"You any good at it?", asked Oren

"Yeah, I guess I'm pretty good", I answered, trying to sound appropriately modest.

"Well, just you remembah", said Oren, "if you ain't the lead sled dog the view never changes."

Like a lot of Oren's "wisdom", I didn't give it much thought at first; but it kept nagging at me: "if you ain't the lead sled dog the view never changes". I finally understood that being the lead sled dog was about winning—the importance of being Number One, running the fastest, taking the lead...that anything else is just following the leaders. Some people say we shouldn't place too much emphasis on winning, that not everyone can be Number One; but I suspect that's more of a comforting rationalization for those caught back in the traces than anything else..

Sometimes those of us in sales need to remember that the business of Selling is in fact the business of Winning...nothing more and nothing less, that's simply all it's about. There is no second place. A true salesperson lives to win, to be Number One, to be the lead sled dog. But it's not just a way of selling, it's a way of living. Consider this: real sales success will come only to those who have successfully focused every single aspect of their lives on winning. That attitude and that commitment is perhaps the single most critical requirement for a salesperson.

Vince Lombardi said it, "winning...it's the only thing". He and Oren were on to something.

TWO-LANE ROADS

Ever since I started writing articles about my authentic "Old Yankee" neighbor, Oren, he's become quite the celebrity up here in New Hampshire. It seems that Oren spends more and more of his time thinking up tidbits of "Yankee Wisdom" for his new fans who seem to hang on his every word. To me at least, most of his tidbits don't make much sense, but every now and then there's an occasional pearl…

Like the other day…

Sitting out on his front porch (complete with old mongrel dog) I remarked to Oren how often I was surprised that people I had met throughout my career—especially casual contacts that had little to do with my business at the time —eventually played an important role in my future. Often they seemed to be there to help me just when I needed it most. "Just shows", I said, "you never know!"

"Well," Oren says, "you musta given 'em some reason t'want t'help yuh. See, it's like this. You got two choices with most everybody—treat 'em good or treat 'em poor and usual you gets right back just about what y'gives, and sometimes a little more."

I said, "What you mean, Oren, is that you better treat everyone like they're important to you, right?"

"Well it seems t'me," says he, "that a fella's life is a lot like a two-lane road. What y'leave behind goin' one way, y'er gonna run right into again on the way back."

I guess in selling, there are no unimportant customers or prospects. In managing there are no unimportant employees. There are no one-way streets.

COURAGE TO CHANGE

Actually it was my mother who said it, referring to my dad's propensity to resist anything new: "Change is like pulling teeth!" He had a hard time with change. Most of us do.

"Don't fix it if it ain't broke!" Traditional yankee wisdom. After all, if what you're doing is working, why change? If you do something new you might get better results...of course, you might get worse ones. So...

"Nothing is resisted as much as change". Just a simple fact , and yet...

"ALL COMPETITIVE ADVANTAGE IS THE RESULT OF CHANGE!"

Do you realize how true that statement is? You release a new product or service–that's change. New pricing–that's change. A new marketing campaign, advertising, a new sales strategy, a new technology such as e-commerce or CRM—all Change!

Here's an example. Suppose you and your company make an excellent product and provide excellent service and support. As a salesperson you do a great job building customer relationships. All of those are your sources of competitive advantage today. Now also suppose that your competitor has decided to take some of that business away from you. How can they do it? The answer is "create change"–offer a new and different product or incentive, launch a new marketing campaign or customer relationship program with a unique "value proposition", leverage a new technology, and so on.

So what does this mean to a salesperson?

Today we're all faced with a tight market, tighter expense budgets, and no less aggressive sales goals. There's increasing pressure to make goals, and that's no less true for our competitors. Every major sales opportunity will be tightly contested! Traditional sales thinking says that we should focus on the basics, do well what we do best, work harder, and not take too many risks. But is that the right strategy?

What we really need today is Competitive Advantage. We need it in order to win new business and to keep the business we have. So perhaps this is exactly the time when we should be looking for new ways to create and deliver customer value, developing higher level customer relationships, using more powerful planning and tracking systems such as CRM.

IF WE DON'T OUR COMPETITORS SURELY WILL!

Interestingly enough, it is in tough times that new market leaders emerge…because they had the courage to create change in the marketplace.

110% EFFORT

A new year is always a good time to spend a few minutes thinking about what we did right last year and what we could have done better.

Unfortunately, if we're honest about it, that "better" list just goes on and on and on and...well, I get tired just thinking about it. This year I'm taking a new tact. I'm going to try and write down a few of the things my customers taught me and I'll try to remember them throughout the new year...

- My customers taught me that they want to be more successful.
- They want to have happier customers.
- They want competitive advantage.
- They want to be more productive, more effective, and more efficient.
- They taught me that my job—as a vendor or supplier of any product or service—is to help them meet these goals!
- They taught me that *"My Opinion of My Service is Always a Little Higher than My Customer's Opinion!"*–

I'm pretty pleased with the job I've done for my clients this last year. I think I've worked hard for them and I personally know all the times I've gone "above and beyond". Still, it comes as a bit of a shock when I realize they're not always overcome with special gratitude. In fact, they believe they got exactly what they paid for!

Conclusion:
It takes 110% effort to gain a 100% satisfied customer!"

WHAT CAN YOU DO WITH A ROPE?

What can you do with a rope? On the whole they're pretty handy things. Most of us have one somewhere around the house, or hanging in a shed, or maybe in the trunk of the car just in case. Ropes come in all lengths and sizes and colors ñ from skinny ones like thread or string to big fat ones the size of your fist. Nylon, cotton, hemp, even steel ñ rope has it all and we just cant say enough good things about rope!

So what can you do with a rope? Just suppose I gave you one right now, any size, length, color you want. What kind of rope is it? What would you use it for? What's the first thing you would think of?

Would it be kite string? Is that what you have in mind today?

Would you use it to tie something on the roof of the car? To hold down a tent? For a clothesline?

Did you think of making a swing with it?

A tug-of war?

Did you imagine tying something up? How about a leash or runner for the dog?

Would you use it to climb a mountain, or to anchor a boat?

Did you make a bridge? Tow a car?

Did you think of walking a tightrope, or were you sewing on a button?

We use ropes to either keep things from getting away from us or to help us get us somewhere or accomplish something. It sort of depends on what you want to do. We make ropes in life too to do the same things.

So, what kind of ropes are you making today?

Are you making ropes to tie things down, to keep things from getting away from you and stop things from changing in your life—to keep what you have? Unfortunately it seems like there is never enough rope, or rope that is strong enough for you to feel really secure

Are you making ropes to take you somewhere? To make bridges, to climb life's mountains, to swing free ? Is your focus on moving to the next step in your career? New or better relationships? New opportunities for business? Are you comfortable knowing that in order to move to new things you might have to let go once in awhile and swing from one rope to another?

The kind of ropes we make depend on how we view the business of life. Life can be a never-ending series of dangers or of opportunities. It has been said that we create our own realities and that turns our to be true. We create them by how we look at life and by the ropes we make that either bind us to our fears or carry us to our dreams.

PART V

ON SUCCESS...IN SALES MANAGE-
MENT

SALES MANAGEMENT REVEILLE

Do we need first-line sales managers anymore? Several recent articles in national magazines pose this question; and more than one "re-engineering theorist" suggests that the sales and marketing re-engineering process will eliminate most sales managers through the empowering of field salespeople as "microbusinesses". In short, traditional salespeople, as employees utilizing virtual office technology, will work as functionally independent small businesses. Technology, not managers, will enable corporations to communicate and track sales progress. Estimates are that for every five managers today only one will be needed in the not-too-distant future.

To the accountants it's perhaps an attractive proposition. Using the technology of customer relationship management, sales organizations are closing expensive remote offices and reducing expensive administrative personnel overhead—with reported bottom line savings of up to 20%. If the definition of sales manager is someone who tracks and manages sales activity, forecasts sales revenues, and does general sales personnel administration, then a valid case can probably be made that far fewer "managers" will soon be necessary. That translates to a significant potential reduction in sales overhead dollars and a real increase in selling margins...and make no mistake, in today's marketplace margins are what it's all about.

Few experienced sales managers would describe their jobs this way, although most would admit that too much time is, in fact, taken up with "adminastrivia". In my seminars and workshops I've asked hundreds of front-line sales managers to identify and prioritize what they consider to be their most important management tasks and roles. On their lists, coaching and motivating are always on the top while activity tracking and administration invariably bring up the rear. So most managers feel their job is to play a significant and necessary role in the sales process...albeit one with more than a few frustrations and headaches. The corporation,

79

however, often takes exactly the reverse view, i.e., first-line management's most important role is tracking, forecasting, and administration. Even sales representatives typically perceive management's primary role not as coach and "mentor" but rather "the sales police".

The problem is one of measurement and perceptions. Just how necessary—and, more importantly, effective—is the sales manager in the selling process? What part of sales revenues can be directly attributed to the guidance of sales management? How much management time is really spent in coaching, motivating, and face-to-face time with customers?

We asked a group of sales people this question: "How effective is the coaching you receive from your manager in helping you close sales?." These were some of the answers:

"Not very. Times have changed since he/she was out in the field!"
"My manager is only concerned with what's going to close this month."
"Coaching? I spend most of my time educating my manager."
"I usually don't hear anything I haven't already thought of."
"Coaching sessions just take time away from selling."
"He/she doesn't know what' going on…and I don't have the time to tell him/her."

The truth lies in understanding just how difficult the job of sales management really is. Most managers are personally focused on helping drive sales and making salespeople more successful—and want to do this through better coaching and mentoring. Millions of dollars are spent by companies each year to train managers to do these tasks better. Despite all the good intentions, however, managers are still too often overwhelmed with administration and have far less knowledge than they need to be effective coaches about "what's really going on out there".

"The only way I know what's really going on in the sales territories is through the call reports I have the reps fill out .. and of course by talking to them. Frankly that's not always a lot of information—and it does take time away from their selling."

As sales re-engineering brings change to sales organizations, much of the change will be in the new customer relationship management systems that not only help salespeople to be more productive and effective but also return real-time sales progress information direct to managers as well as to the corporation. This creates new paradigms for management:

1. Far fewer sales managers will be needed to track and monitor sales activities.

2. Managers will have the information available they need to be more effective coaches...without the necessity of cumbersome and time consuming manual call reports, forecasts, and "how's it going?" sessions with the salespeople.

3. Sales managers will become accountable .. the justification for their position will be in whether he or she provides a clear and definable return-on-investment to the sales representatives.

4. The 90% job of the new sales manager is Coach.

If that were all there was to it then it would be easy, i.e., managers armed with better information must spend more of their time coaching, in the field, and with customers...and salespeople need to perceive value from this. It is, unfortunately, not that simple. Traditional sales coaching and motivational techniques will prove to be painfully inadequate— "Here's an idea you might try" won't cut it anymore. The "high-value" manager will have become a master strategist, a sales resource armed with a broad base of information, experience, and outstanding strategic planning skills—a manager who is continuously monitoring trends, sales progress, and competitive activity. The analogy is not unlike a modern general who directs the course of battle using advanced C3I (command, control, communication and intelligence) technology that provides real-time battlefield information.

The general-of the-army analogy is helpful in another way as well. It's one thing to have information available, but it's entirely another thing to know how to use it most effectively. No general takes charge without a firm grounding in military strategies and tactics. The "new breed" of sales manager is going to need a "war college" education that few, if any, have received to date.

In the new sales environment, the only purpose and justification of management is to provide clear and measurable added value to the salesperson…nothing more and nothing less. It is about creating a new sales/sales management partnership of strategies and tactics that deliver more sales revenues with higher margins in less time. It is ultimately a new role for managers with potentially greater challenges and rewards than ever before.

It's all about surviving and succeeding in the new management environment—developing a focus on strategies as well as tactics, creating a new value-based selling model for greater competitive advantage, and new management coaching and development techniques that, when combined with today's enabling technologies, make the sales manager the most valuable resource in the selling equation.

HIRING WINNERS!

It's no secret. The greatest responsibility of sales management is hiring sales winners. It's not easy. When you first become a sales manager you're faced with the fact that you can't do sell every deal yourself; you have to rely, as painful as it may be, on the salespeople. (Unfortunately some managers never learn this–a sure route to an ulcer!). Your future is, for better or worse, in their hands.

There are characteristics that all sales "winners" ("good hands" people) seem to have in common. So try looking for these in your next interview:

1. **Persuasion**—sales winners have an innate need to persuade others to their point of view. They treat a job interview just like a sales call—they need to win! In the interview they ask you your needs, clearly present their personal "features and benefits", handle objections, and—above all–close for the offer!

2. **Empathy**—sales winners accurately hear what others say and sense what they mean. Ask an interviewee to feed back their understanding of what you've been telling them about the kind of rep you want to hire for the job. See whether they "get it" or their stuck on their personal agenda.

3. **Decision-Makers**–a sales winner knows where he or she wants to go in their career and can tell you specifically how they've worked to date to achieve their goals. Decision-makers don't rely on "dumb luck" or even "hard work" for success. They have a history of "making it happen" by themselves.

4. **Leadership**—leaders in sales are also leaders in their personal life…always! Ask potential hires how they exhibit leadership outside work.

5. **Busy People**—sales winners are busy people—at work, at home, in the community. In fact they're so busy you may wonder where they find the time for selling! Busy people know how to manage time and priorities for success in everything they do

Hiring salespeople with these characteristics is better than a whole bottle of Pepto!

KNOW THY SALES FORCE

I am continually amazed by the *new technologies of selling*. Laptops, note-books, sub-notebooks, PDA's, wireless. Email, The Web...and on and on it goes. I'm also a little skeptical. Sometimes I wonder—in the quest to make more and more capabilities and information instantly available to salespeople—if we're getting way ahead of ourselves. In other words, are we doing things just because we can, technically speaking; or because we know these things can really help salespeople sell? I suspect there's some of the former out there.

The companies who appear to be getting the most benefit from technology today are not necessarily the most technically sophisticated or the most visionary. They are the ones who truly understand the real, day-to-day *obstacles* their salespeople face and have worked with them effectively to find realistic *solutions* to overcome those obstacles...some using technology and some not! This sounds simple but may be one of the most difficult tasks in business. In many organizations there is an increasingly broad gulf between corporate and the field.

As once sales executive told me, "If you're not careful, you fall in love with technology. Then you don't really communicate with your sales reps and you can end up finding elegant solutions for non-existent problems...and create more problems than you had when you started!"

Before you automate your sales force—or do anything else—try completing this statement:

"I know our salespeople could sell more if they could..."

Now *that's* what you want to focus on. The answer might be found in technology, or in re-engineering your sales process, or in marketing, or management, or most likely in some combination of all of these. In other words, before you do anything remember this "commandment" of sales management...

Know thy Sales Force!

THE PROFIT'S THE THING!

In most of the companies I consult to, we spend a lot of time talking about helping salespeople make their sales quotas–sales *revenue* quotas. When I was a company salesman, that's what I thought about too. Once I started my own business, however, that changed.

Day to day, to tell you the truth, I don't give much thought (if any) to my business revenue. The only thing I care about is how much money I walk away with when all is said and done–in other words, *profit*. I mean, you can't spend *revenue*!

My business, of course, is no different than any other. Every corporate executive–and certainly every stockholder or investor—understands that difference between revenue and profits. What I'm confused about is why we goal and pay salespeople on revenues. This seems like a fundamental "disconnect".

For example, no company really likes to discount it's prices because in doing so we're reducing profit margins. A revenue-goaled salesperson, however, only sees the problem in terms of sales volume to make quota. In my own business, when I "negotiate" price, I view it in terms of whether winning the business is worth my time and effort for the profits I'll make. So I sell my "Value" to justify the price I want to charge and the profit I want to make.

Perhaps there's something I'm missing, but it seems to me that it would make a lot more sense to goal and pay salespeople on gross profits contribution. It's the surest way I know to change a sales rep's perspective on excessive discounting and selling Value.

READING & WRITING

It's getting harder to find good salespeople. I hear that from more and more personnel recruiters. It's not just finding experienced, successful salespeople, it's also finding good, young, talented people with real potential for sales success. Why should it be so hard to find the salespeople of the future? Is it the today's college graduates aren't interested in a sales career?

The interest hasn't changed; it's that sales recruiters are looking for more than many of today's applicants offer. To be more specific, recruiters tell me that all too many of the young candidates they see lack basic verbal skills. They are unable to express themselves orally and in writing sufficiently to meet the requirements of a sales career. In other words, they can't read and write on anything close to a "professional" level.

I have two of my children in high school. It seems to me that today's educational focus worries more about developing their mathematical skills than their verbal abilities. Certainly math scores seem to count for more for college admission than the ability to read, write, and speak clearly. Now please understand that I am not against math—even though I still get night sweats remembering algebra. Math is especially in today's world of technology.

Recently, however, I was asked to observe a public speaking class at a high school, and to provide the students some feedback on their presentations. Many had excellent delivery style which would have been fine had it not been for the *horrendous* grammar and misuse of the English language. It made me crazy that no one—not even the teacher—seemed to think this was a problem!

It has been my observation, without fail, that people who read constantly and can express themselves clearly both orally and on paper tend to do well whatever their careers—and do well in their lives!

No matter what a persons career or field of endeavor—salesperson or engineer—the ability to communicate effectively, persuasively, and clearly is fundamental. It's one set of basics we need to get back to—and fast!

REMODELING ADVICE...

We've been having a lot of remodeling construction done around the house the last few weeks. Whole new kitchen and hallway and an addition off the back of the house. It's gotten so bad that I've had to move my office to the only quiet room left: the downstairs bathroom. It's cramped but it's not so bad really. I've got my cordless phone and my notebook computer; and in it's own way it is, well,...convenient.

In any case, David is one of the young men working on our kitchen and an exceptionally talented carpenter. He told me this morning that someday he's planning to leave his current employer and start his own home remodeling business. It was awkward for him but he asked me if I would be willing to be a reference for him when he starts up.

David has worked for Mike for a number of years now; and Mike has been good to him. He's taught David his craft and paid him more than fairly...and Mike is a good guy to work for. So David tells me he's feeling pretty guilty about becoming Mike's competitor...and especially about asking me to be his reference. It's understandable.

I gave David his first piece of business advice, one that I hope he'll remember for a long time. *"David, always hire people who will become good enough to become your strongest competitor!"*

You see, Mike is successful today because he hires people like David. Having David as his competitor won't really hurt Mike. It *will* hurt all those other "weak sisters" in the market who don't know enough to hire and grow their future competition.

Let's all wish David luck!...

IT'S THE CLOSING RATIO!

Sales Managers: what should you be managing today with your sales people?

Sales Calls/Day or Week? Clearly a certain level of activity is fundamental to creating sales but measuring activity is a poor indicator of success? It also doesn't tell us much about "sales efficiency".

The only resource a salesperson has is time. That time can be spent on opportunities that produce business or on opportunities that don't, i.e., wins, losses, and things that just never happen. The key is to measure how much of a rep's time is spent on "wins" and how to increase it!

Do you know your rep's actual closing ratios. A 1:3 (wins to loss/other) is generally considered good in most industries. In my experience I've found more than one manager who assumed his reps had this kind of ratio or better—only to find out that the reality was 1 in 8 or 9.

How important is this? Calculate the increased sales revenue of a rep improving his or her closing ratio from, say, 1:5 to just 1:4 assuming the same amount of opportunities. The results can be staggering!

How do you improve closing ratios? Make sure your reps are spending their time where they can win, not just on "big deals"; and coach their sales strategies to make sure they're the best they can be!

MANAGING LITTLE LEAGUE

Sales management is, of course, a great deal more than a series of strategies or techniques or methodologies. It is still about people—specifically salespeople—and about management's ability to motivate and guide them to success. If it were only that easy! Techniques and methods work best when management has the fundamental ability to lead effectively through change. Ultimately change is what we have been talking about—change in the market, change in customer expectations and perceptions, change in finding new ways to do the job of selling. Unfortunately, no technique or method can be effective unless the impact of change (i.e., resistance to new things) can be managed.

What does it take then to be a leader; to develop the trust and confidence of the salespeople, to guide them through the often painful (but necessary) process of accepting and adopting new and better ways of selling? Well, everything that I know about sales leadership—at least the important things—I learned from a bunch of nine-year-olds. Now, I feel a little embarrassed admitting that considering all the management courses I've attended; but it seemed like I always came back from those classes fired up with new ideas and techniques guaranteed to make me a great sales manager, more or less. Six months later I was still in the less category. It's been frustrating...

My nine year olds were little league baseball players. It may sound funny, but I used to wonder why I couldn't be as effective a sales manager as I was a little league coach. I'd been roped into little league some ten years ago by my son, Casey ("Gee, Dad, our team really needs a coach..."); and considering that I know about as much about baseball as I do about differential calculus (I think that's an auto part or something), I did a respectable job of it. In fact, on the ball field I actually did all the things I've heard about in sales manager's school—I motivated; I coached;

I strategized; we won games; everybody was happy and somehow it all worked.

Unfortunately, the non-existent pay plan for little league managers dictated that I continue in sales management for the foreseeable future. Fortunately, however, I did learn four key principles of sales management from all those years at the sandlot…and to quote the poet, Robert Frost, "that has made all the difference".

*   *   *   *   *

I: Who Wins the Game?

Let me tell you about Chris. Nice guy. Coach of the Little League "Orioles" last year, but no kid wants to be on his teams. Very confused; I suspect he thinks this is real major league baseball, and I'm not sure if I pressed him that he could tell the difference between the ball diamond behind the elementary school and Fenway Park. Chris gets all worked up during every game and spends a lot of time yelling at his team. It gets ugly when the Orioles are losing. I think Chris is confused about who really wins the game.

Now I've gotten worked up a time or two myself. I even got thrown out of a game once for arguing with an umpire and kicking dirt on his shoes. (I'm not real proud of it—the umpire was 13 and had on brand new Reeboks). My point isn't that Chris shouldn't be that upset over the game. It's that he needs to stop taking winning or losing so personally—he's hurting his players more than he's helping them. They know they'll never play as well as Chris would if he was out there. Chris doesn't understand that a manager is not a player. Only players can play the game and only players can win or lose. The manager's only job is to help the players win—and to win himself at managing!.

Sometimes the hardest thing for a sales manager to accept is that he or she is no longer in the game—a player, a sales representative. We no longer get to win or lose at selling. We can become winners only in the game of management. Think of it this way: if the true objective of the salesperson is to make sure the customer wins, then the objective of the sales manager is to make sure the reps win. In short, we're out of the game, kicked upstairs, and not allowed out on the field of play with the customers—except when invited or to give some advice or encouragement. We get to pick the team, create the game plan, and send in plays...that's about it. We can't do the sales job for them.

Who wins the game? The sales reps...and hopefully their customers!

II: You Gotta Have A Game Plan!

Bernie is a baseball coach...a professional. He coaches the JV team over at the high school and gets paid for it, so I guess that makes him a "pro". I met him a few years into my "coaching experience" when Casey turned 14 and Bernie and I coached the "Pirates" together. Managing little kids was easy compared to teenagers. With little kids you teach them how to hit, where to stand, tell them when to run, where to throw the ball and encourage them a lot. They need, want and expect to be told what to do—and some percentage of the time will actually do it. Teenagers however, have a different agenda; they don't want to be bothered with "rookie" basics. According the Bernie, "You don't really direct experienced play-ers—the best you can do is kinda point 'em in the right direction and herd 'em that way. They'll head pretty much there if they think you know what you're talkin' about". In other words, with experienced players don't try to lead them by always focusing on basic skills and tactics; "herd" them in the right direction by having a "Game Plan".

It has often amazed me how much salespeople are like my baseball play-ers. Sales trainees and relatively inexperienced sales reps really need—and want—coaching to develop solid skills. At that stage of their development they need to be continuously trained and reminded of what we think of as "the basics". Most sales managers are really pretty comfortable with this kind of managing and coaching, if only because those skills are firmly established and come easily. But salespeople, like little leaguers, someday grow up to become "experienced sales professionals" who are looking for their managers to provide something more: a "Game Plan" for success. "Give me the strategy, Boss; call in a play when you see a way to do things better; and let me do the rest!" .

For many of us then, the coaching and managing skills with which we're the most familiar and know how to use the best don't really apply to the most important—and highest producing—segment of our sales force. Ask yourself this question: "Do my most experienced people think that I have a real game plan for success? If so, could they tell me what it is?" An effective manager needs to become a chameleon—leading young salespeople with solid tactical coaching and leading the experienced with a solid game plan, sending in plays tactics as the sale progresses, and letting the sales reps execute. In short, if you want to manage the "pros", "Ya gotta have a Game Plan!"

III: Play the Bench

Have you ever seen a little league team on which the "good" players seem to always be in the game (and get all the attention) while the "benchwarmers" play only for the minimum time required? It's sort of generally accepted that if he wants to win the game, the coach really has to play the "stars". I never gave it much thought until we were driving home after a game and Casey asked me how the kids on the bench would ever get any better if they never got to play. Good question. From that I learned to refocus my coaching efforts towards the kids that needed me.

There's a "bench" in every sales organization too, and it's filled by good, average salespeople. They're not failures (those get cleared out pretty quickly). No, the "bench reps" are the ones who do their job consistently, steadily, and reliably but without a lot of fireworks and fanfare…and they usually don't get a lot of management attention. It's not surprising then that management likes to apply itself to the "sales stars" who can deliver the big deals, make the big plays, can put the organization "over the top" in the race for quota...and gives them the lion's share of management time. Besides which, sales managers (all ex-stars themselves) have a lot more in common with the "stars" than the "bench". By most standards, managing the "bench" just isn't near as much fun as working with the "stars"! The truth is, however, that our "stars" need the least amount of our time.

The most successful sales organizations—like the best teams—are not the ones with the most stars but rather those with the greatest depth. i.e., the strongest bench. To develop it sales managers need to refocus their time to play the bench.

IV: You Need the Right Equipment to Win

Nine-year old Joey was a good little ball player whose Dad had once made all-state in high school. Dad willed Joey his personal championship glove and home-run hitting wooden bat...and Joey's determined to use them and be "just like Dad". But times have changed and Joey won't even be competitive...and it's Dad's fault.

Yes, even Little League has gone high-tech. Gloves are bigger, with deeper pockets; and catching a ball has gotten easier. Bats have changed too because aluminum ones hit farther (and the newest, made of carbon-graphite hit farther still—just ask my other son, Tim, who had to have one for his last birthday. Joey simply can't be fully competitive with out-of-date equipment no matter how much talent he has—he'll be consistently out-played. So unfortunately, what was good enough for Dad isn't good enough for Joey—and understanding that may be difficult for both of them.

The "Equipment" of selling has also changed. Notebook computers running customer relationship management software, on-line marketing encyclopedias, remote fax technology, product configurators, cellular phones and wireless data communications, territory mapping and analysis software—these are only a few of the tools which have proven to not only increase the productivity of salespeople but also their sales effectiveness. In short, automated salespeople have the ability to outsell their non-automated (and perhaps even more talented) competitors. They have the advantage of technology to help them provide better customer responsiveness and service and to more tightly focus their marketing and sales efforts.

A "problem" is that sales managers can be a lot like Joe's dad. We know what worked for us as sales reps and we're most comfortable managing reps to work the same way. So salesperson Joe and his sales manager "Dad" may both find it difficult to adjust to this change and may delay upgrading their "selling equipment" until it's too late. As in baseball, the best equipment is no guarantee of winning, but among competitors, when all other things are equal, the best equipment becomes a source of advantage.

*   *   *   *   *

Putting it all together, it's the simple concept that a sales manager isn't a "designated hitter" or "clean-up" batter on the sales team. He or she is a resource provider, a mentor, an advisor. The job is making sales winners, not being one. The job is assuring that salespeople have the tools they need for competitive advantage—equipment, skills, and a strategy—or "game plan"—for success!

That's Big League Management in the Little League!

HOW TO BE A GREAT
SALES MANAGER

It's not easy to be a sales manager these days–even harder to be a GREAT sales manager. Here's some key strategies for those aspiring to greatness...

1. Make your Salespeople your Customers–that's right, your customers because that's exactly what they are! Your success is totally dependent upon their success. Give them the same kind of care and feeding you would give your company's very best customer. Become their "Success Coach".

2. Manage Perception -too many sales managers are viewed as "Gotcha!" managers by their reps. In other words, the reps feel that the sales manager is to monitor and correct their performance–not be their success coach!

3. Be a Company Executive–one of the best ways a sales manager can help his or her reps is by positioning themselves as a company executive who can comfortably meet and work with the customer's executive staff and who can create business-to-business relationships.

4. Make your Salespeople into Businesspeople–investing in sales skill training is always a good idea BUT you may also want to spend some of your training dollars and time on developing your rep's understanding of business principles and the types of issues customers face today.

5. The Plan is the Thing–do your salespeople have a detailed Territory Business Plan? Have they selected the optimum accounts to call on with the highest potential and profitability? Do they have solid strategies in place for key competitors and to successfully address the obstacles they face? If not, maybe they're "wandering" the territory and accounts hoping to stumble upon opportunity.

A great sales manager is a venture capitalist who views each salesperson as an investment business—a VC who assures that each "business" or territory has an effective plan in place, that the plan is well executed, and that the business/rep has the right skills, knowledge, and resources for success. Our manager/VC is an advisor and success coach focused upon each of his/her investments becoming a success—and who shares personally in that success.

PART VI

ON TECHNOLOGY, PROCESS, ...AND THE FUTURE OF SELLING

21st CENTURY SELLING–THE SEARCH FOR COMPETITIVE ADVANTAGE

Taking selling to its most basic component: selling is the search for Competitive Advantage. I have asked hundreds of salespeople this simple question: "Do you sell more when you have competitive advantage? ". The obvious answer is " Yes " with this one proviso: " As long as you can create it in the mind of the customer."

As we look into the new century—and what selling will be like here—we may find that what has changed more than anything else is the mind of the customer. In other words, our challenge as salespeople will be to understand a new set of customer attitudes and buying patterns that will impact how we sell, what we sell, and just how successful we are.

Our culture and our society has changed more in the last 50 years than perhaps in all of recorded history. When I was a young boy I remember hearing about what the world of the year 2000 would look like. We expected weekend trips to the moon, robots would serve us, we would all wear wrist radios and televisions, and commute to work in personal flying machines. Well, we didn't perhaps achieve all of those, but the world of 2000 is still pretty amazing.

Whoever dreamed of personal computers? Of the internet? Of cellular telephones in everyone's pocket? Even microwave ovens? But perhaps more than anything else the 21st century world is a world of communications.

The wonder of communications is hardly a wonder anymore…except to those of us old enough to remember rotary dial telephones, operator-assisted long distance, or radio. My children take the "wonders" of world-wide live television on 120 channels and the internet as a normal part of life. As for me, I'm still amazed by a direct dial long distance call between Europe and the States.

Last Saturday morning my son woke me from a sound sleep to tell me I had a phone call from someone in Kuala Lumpur.

"Kuala Lumpur? Kuala Lumpur where?", I croaked.

"You know, Dad, it's over near China." (No big deal).

So we fax and email with our computers and cellular phones. We access vast troves of information on anything with the click of a button. No piece of data is too arcane, no idea too obscure, no place too remote that it cannot traveled to electronically in milliseconds.

What is the attraction of all this communications technology? Are we developing a more educated, literate, and better informed society because of it? Probably not. The real attraction is more likely its immediacy. In other words, those who seek information can find it quicker and faster and in greater quantities than ever before. We can reach out to instantly contact almost anyone worldwide in moments. We can research and purchase more and more products and services without ever leaving home. So the attraction is perhaps more a reflection of today's high-speed, instant-gratification society than anything else.

Without ever leaving home… the workplace is being restructured as the virtual office, "telecommuting" electronically from an "office" in the home. Webcasting and Conferencing. The social "chat" capabilities of the internet are creating virtual communities with worldwide members who will likely never meet in person…or need to. Customer buying patterns are changing as well. Just a few years ago, it would have been unthinkable for a company to purchase business products from a catalog or from a telephone sales person. No longer, however. Today both individuals and businesses regularly use catalog, telephone sales, computers and the internet (and even television) routinely to make major purchases.

What this all means is that today's customer is not absolutely sure that he or she really needs a salesperson to call—especially if the customer feels that the purpose of that salesperson is just to present product features and then use their sales skills to pressure the customer into buying. Many customers are also realizing that the products and services they need can often be purchased at a lower price when an outside salesperson is not involved. In short, the days of the salesperson who relies on product, price, and sales skills to create competitive advantage may well be numbered. So, if not this, what then is the future of the outside salesperson and where will his or her competitive advantage come from?

We asked a group of executives why they needed the best salespeople with whom they worked. These were the characteristics and skills they most valued:

1. **Solving problems: the best salespeople had a strong knowledge of their customers business, goals, and challenges, and so were often able to actively help the customer address real business issues.**

2. **Avoiding problems: the best salespeople were able to help their customer look down the road ahead, anticipate changing needs, and avoid problems before they became business issues.**

3. **Leap the " Application Gap ": the best salespeople worked in partnership with their customers, helping them to apply the salesperson's product or service in order to gain the maximum results possible from it.**

Each executive felt that the salesperson who provided these kinds of services was worth paying a price differential. In addition, few expressed any interest in looking at competitive products even though they were told that those products might offer additional features or a lower price. In the mind of these customers, salespeople with these three characteristics had established true competitive advantage.

The challenge for sales organizations will be to develop this kind of salesperson-one who still has excellent selling skills and thorough product knowledge but who is capable of developing a true partnership relationship with the customers. That relationship will be based upon the expertise of the salesperson and the contribution he or she can make to the success of the customer's business.

The first step will be providing salespeople with enhanced tools and capabilities. We will need to develop their overall business expertise and industry knowledge. In other words, knowing your own company and product is half the job. We must provide them with access to more extensive and complete customer and clean market information- and the technology tools to use that data to make better sales decisions for themselves and their customers. Perhaps the most difficult task, however, will be changing how they view the job of selling.

This kind of 21st century selling model looks for a new breed of salesperson-one who is genuinely interested in the customer's world and as a tireless curiosity about it. That salesperson views his/her success as a result of the customer's success. There is a question which I often ask salespeople, the answer to which rather clearly defines how well they fit this model:

"Would Your Customer Hire You or Your Company As A Consultant If You No Longer Had Your Product to Sell?"

The answer to this question clearly identifies whether a customer views a salesperson and the company he or she represents as partners in business success or only as a provider of a product.

As we sit at the beginning of the new century, there is a unique opportunity for sales organizations to redesign and redefine themselves to this powerful model for new competitive advantage. Doing so may require sailing some new and uncharted waters.

The American poet, Robert Frost, wrote, " I took the road less traveled and that has made all the difference". In tomorrow's marketplace, the road less traveled is also the road less certain; despite that, it is also where all the greatest opportunities lie.

I HATE MY LAPTOP

I hate my laptop.

Okay, actually it's a *notebook* computer. Call it anything you want, I call it *heavy*! It's true that they've gotten much lighter than they used to be, but by the time you load up dual batteries, the AC adapter, and all the other "stuff" in your briefcase, the #*!!? thing is *heavy*! (I've been told that the permanent strap marks in my shoulder—and the slight lean—are very attractive…) My doctor says I'm in great shape and asked me about my exercise program. I told him I carry computers thru airports. He doesn't understand…

You know what else I hate? It takes *forever* to boot up and get to anything! Like when a customer asks "Can we meet on the 21st?". You fire up the old laptop (because that's where you keep your calendar); you wait, wait, and wait; only to find the battery is low. So you whip out the AC adapter cord and say to your customer "Do you mind if I crawl under your desk to plug this in?".

Then there's airport security. "Is that a computer, sir?" (No, it's a barbell.) "Could you start it up, please?" (Uh, oh…battery's dead, won't start. Security people think that's suspicious). "You can plug it in over there." (No "sir" anymore. Waves to armed guard to watch me "just in case". Why can't I find the AC adapter?? Did I pack it in the bag I checked?).

Let's say it all together, Road Warriors: *Been There, Done That!*.

Computer manufacturers of the world, hear our plea! Fill your notebook cases with helium! Give me "instant on"! Give me "solar" power or batteries that last longer than the Energizer bunny! I need my laptop but one of us is going to kill the other before long…

CUSTOMER RELATIONSHIP MANAGEMENT–THE NEXT CHAPTER

What is the future of Customer Relationship Management? Will it become the indispensable sales tool? A "must have" for every salesperson? Beginning as a Contact and Account Management tool, many of today's systems have evolved to enterprise-wide Opportunity Management Systems (OMS). Where are we going next–what is "the next chapter" in CRM and CRM?

Customer relationship management. Enterprise-wide CRM. Quite possibly the most exciting idea to hit the business of selling in the last 50 years. Virtually everyone agrees its potential value to salespeople and sales organizations is enormous–at least in theory. As analysts project a multi-billion dollar marketplace by the year 2000, a thousand software vendors race for leadership. It would sound like an investor's dream except that the fundamental problems that have plagued CRM and CRM (customer relationship management) since its beginnings some 15 years ago are still there. CRM's problems can be condensed into this single statement: many salespeople just won't use it. Why? The simple answer is that, bottom line, they do not believe that customer relationship management just does enough for them personally to justify the additional time and effort it requires. In other words, they do not believe CRM will actively help them sell significantly more! This is no secret to the software vendors who have added volumes of new features and capabilities with each release. Still, it doesn't seem to be enough–and sometimes has the opposite effect.

Instead of looking at CRM features, let's look at selling. What is it that helps salespeople sell more?

(1) Salespeople sell more when they can create competitive advantage in their territory/market for their products and services, i.e. find and win the best opportunities.

(2) Salespeople sell more when they effectively manage the Customer Relationship

(3) Salespeople sell more when they can do their job more efficiently and make fewer mistakes, i.e. missed appointments and follow ups, and so forth.

Improving Efficiency, Productivity and The Customer Relationship.

To date, customer relationship management has focused far more on the second and third of these–efficiencies, productivity improvement, and managing the customer relationship—than the first; and therein lies much of the problem. CRM began with Contact Managers (a personal information tool), progressed to tracking Accounts as well as contacts, and finally to enterprise-wide Opportunity Management Systems. Fundamentally, however, CRM in any form, is still a giant database used for recording account/opportunity/contact profiles, tracking contacts and relationship history, measuring opportunity progress, logging sales activities, and perhaps delivering leads. Features such as "To Do" managers and calendars are nice tools, but using a laptop computer is a painfully slow and often impractical way to manage them.

All this "tracking" information of course is a goldmine for managers and marketing departments—and it can help a sales rep—but it just doesn't do all that much for a salesperson's "sell more" goals. But even the best "Opportunity Management" software isn't of much use if it's not helping manage or leverage the best sales opportunities in the salesperson's territory!

Creating Competitive Advantage

Let's go back to Goal #1: Establish Competitive Market Advantage and Find & Win the Best Opportunities. Other than by Product or Price advantage, how can a sales rep create competitive advantage in his or her territory? How can he or she consistently find the sales opportunities–the ones that will close the quickest and easiest, result in the highest customer satisfaction, and offer the best return-on-investment, i.e. require the least price discounting?

In simplest terms, a salesperson needs to work a territory business marketing plan to help him or her make better sales decisions. This plan pulls together comprehensive territory and account knowledge, competitive data, product information, customer history, and customer relationship information. From this the salesperson can:

> set realistic and achievable goals and objectives,
> - accurately assess his/her market position, competitor's strategies and strengths/weaknesses,
> - determine the competitive niche in which he or she can win and develop effective competitive strategies
> - identify the highest potential accounts and opportunities,
> - create key account strategies,
> - develop specific, executable sales tactics
> - plan how his or her most valuable resource–Time–can be best spent for maximum return on investment.

All this goes well before ever starting to make sales calls and is a continuous, constant process of evaluation and reevaluation. In other words, a salesperson needs to functionally act as a small business–a business with a plan. Wandering the territory making great sales calls, following up leads, hoping for "a hot one" isn't going to cut it alone anymore.

I can gain advantage over my competitor by having a better business plan because from that plan I can develop more effective sales approaches, identify higher potential accounts, and optimize my time–all of which means "sell more". We call this approach SSTM (Strategic Sales Territory Management)–and believe it's integration into CRM technology will be the next chapter in the evolution of customer relationship management.

SSTM or "Customer Relationship Management"?

Another school of thought projects that the next generation of customer relationship management technology will focus on enhanced Customer Relationship Management (CRM). While not mutually exclusive from the SSTM territory management model, the CRM model projects that the greatest value of CRM will be found it it's abilities to help salespeople and sales organizations better serve the customer and enhance the supplier/buyer relationship. Keeping in mind, however, that "value" lies in the eyes of the customer, the future direction of customer relationship management must depend upon what salespeople (the true customer) believe will help them the most to sell more.

In working with thousands of salespeople in the last few years, it is our experience that, rightly or wrongly, the vast majority believes that they have very good customer relationships. In other words, neither they nor their managers feel that "relationships" are significantly standing in the way of sales success. No one is against the idea of using CRM as a tool to build stronger customer relationships, but many salespeople question if it is really needed and worth their effort.

What do salespeople believe is the biggest obstacle to their success? Without exception the answer is Time Utilization. For every sales rep, time is a limited resource. Sales quotas increase with each new year, but available time does not. The decisions each salesperson must make each and every day are these–questions that can only be answered by salespeople who know their business, have needed information at hand, and have a sales territory plan in place:

- What is the best use of my selling time right now?
- Where can I find the best return on my time investment?

- What is the best thing I can do next to most effectively advance each of my sales opportunities closer to the Close?
- Have I planned for all the "what if's" of selling?

The point is that salespeople believe the ability to effectively answer these questions is in fact worth a reasonable investment of their time and can help them sell more. The SSTM approach can address each of these and so–from the viewpoint of the customer–may represent the best future for Customer relationship management.

An CRM Architecture for SSTM

Using a territory business plan as a competitive advantage tool isn't a new idea but the capability to do it effectively and relatively easy is! Consider the difficulty (and time needed) to manually collect, collate, and analyze the amounts of data needed in a manual, paper-based sales planning system. Add to that the frustration (and time needed) to constantly update and re-analyze all that paperwork. Territory business planning has always been a good idea with three problems: (1) little information availability, (2) excessive time required, and (3) most salespeople were never trained to run a business–they were trained to make sales calls!

Customer relationship management today can directly address #1 and #2. CRM can collect and deliver the needed business planning information from virtually unlimited sources and analyze data in a mere fraction of the time needed to do it by hand. The only thing missing is integrating #3: the business plan process itself

Keep in mind that a customer relationship management system, by itself, is only an information database and communications infrastructure. To utilize it as a decision-making tool requires the addition and integration of external business planning and analysis processes: methodologies for territory analysis and planning, key account planning, opportunity assessment, and for the creation of sales strategies and tactics. It is an interesting paradox that automating these business planning processes makes them a more valuable tool for the sales force; and at the same time makes customer relationship management a tool worth using.

Organizations implementing customer relationship management will face challenges, which must be addressed and completed in this specific order:

1. Develop comprehensive business planning processes or methodologies for Territory Business Management, Key Account Planning, & Opportunity Management.

2. Develop salespeople and sales managers as "business people" who know how to use process + information + their sales skills in order to make better business decisions.

3. Select a customer relationship management vendor based upon their ability to integrate or "mirror" these processes within their software product.

SALES MANAGERS...THE MISSING LINK IN CUSTOMER RELATIONSHIP MANAGEMENT

Here's the question: "What makes the difference between real success in Customer relationship management and just "ho-hum" results? The answer surprisingly is actually not What but Who. When all the databases have been defined and loaded, when all the laptops have been rolled out to the sales force, there is one critical, overriding success factor left: First line Sales Managers. The final success or failure of a CRM effort rests solidly upon their shoulders and ultimately they will determine just how effectively customer relationship management is used by the sales force. Missing the sales managers is the surest way to "miss the boat" in customer relationship management, and yet their role is too often overlooked. Here is a new "bottom-line" for customer relationship management from a management perspective—first, the essential role of sales managers in a CRM rollout; and second, the tasks before them to assure success.

Customer relationship management—"People-Driven" Systems

*   *   *   *   *

The question of whether customer relationship management is really worth doing or can significantly improve sales efficiency and productivity (read that revenues and profits) has already been asked and debated, and the answer is pretty much: "Well, sometimes it does and sometimes it doesn't".

Still, most companies, especially larger ones, either have some level of customer relationship management or are well down the path of seriously looking at it. Some say, "It's the best thing we ever did!"; and others,

"Well, it didn't do as much as we hoped". Nonetheless, just about everybody in business agrees it's probably a good idea with tremendous potential...if it's done right. And there's the rub, what is "right"—and is there even a single answer? If so, who's got it?

To look for answers we really need to quit thinking of customer relationship management (CRM) as a computer application. Let's just ignore all that technology for a moment. Sure, there's a wealth of hardware and software here, but CRM is very unlike any traditional computer application or system ever created. Customer relationship management is people-driven not technology-driven.

CRM's task is to enhance the activities of people and organizations who sell and support products. Unfortunately other than that, these people and organizations may have almost nothing in common in how they work, plan or manage their businesses. Here in the real world of selling there are few fundamental fixed processes or methodologies like we find in accounting or manufacturing—ones that apply and standardize the majority of work tasks. Instead there are thousands of salespeople, each doing their own jobs in pretty much their own way—or at least in the way their particular organization has decided. Instead of using mostly objective "hard" facts and figures to make decisions, salespeople deal with subjective "what if's", relationships, strategies and tactics. Customer and prospect information is only a tool to help decide on the "best next" course of action to take to close or advance a sale. Customer relationship management works beautifully when people know how to use it in this way to support and really improve what they already do. It works less well when it becomes another corporate system—a data collector.

It would seem at first glance then that it's really the salespeople who are going to determine if CRM is a success or failure. Will they perceive it as a powerful tool to enhance their work, to help them make more money...or will they stick with the comfortable "tried and true" methods of selling? How are we to create an automated sales force who not only uses CRM but pushes it to its maximum potential?

"Sounds like we need to do a real selling job on our salespeople if we want customer relationship management to work!"

Well, that's one idea. But what do you do if not everyone agrees (and they won't!)? Is it still worth automating if some use it and some don't? Then what?

The 100% Solution

Some companies' solution has been, "Don't automate the sales managers. Avoid the Big Brother mentality. Give automation to the salespeople first. Let them get comfortable." One such company reported, after the first year, that over 60% of their salespeople were still actively using the customer relationship management system—and counted this a success story. But was it?

Let's assume that the automated 60% of the sales reps experienced in the first year at least some increase in their personal sales productivity and revenues. That's certainly good; but unfortunately the Company missed the real CRM payoff: The 100% Solution—the ability to utilize comprehensive field sales data to fine-tune the corporate sales and marketing effort for better competitive advantage. Automation's greatest benefits and best return on investment happen when CRM not only helps salespeople sell day-to-day, but also when it provides solutions to an organization's business issues. Competitive advantage in the marketplace can come from developing sharper lead and pipeline management, or team selling, from more accurate forecasting and competitive intelligence, or from better global territory management, as well as from improving unit and individual sales productivity. These "large-scale" benefits, however, are only possible when CRM creates a Corporate sales knowledge-base of accurate, reliable, and complete field sales activity data, rolled up and collected in a single master database. To create that "knowledge-base"—and "The Big Payoff"—will simply require 100% use of CRM by the sales force.

The problem, then with the "Let the reps try it; they'll like it!" approach is that the "Big Payoff" may never be achieved. Even though the number of salespeople using CRM might increase over time, it will never quite get to 100%. There will always be someone who doesn't feel it works for them. In short, "selling" the reps on automation's benefits isn't going to be enough!

Corporate Disconnect

"Why are we automating sales? It's not just a matter of success, it's a matter of survival!" "Here at corporate, there's three questions we can't answer…only you in the field have the answers."

1.) Who are our customers? (You know them, but we only have names of companies.)

2.) Why do they buy? (What are the real reasons? Price? Performance?)

3.) Why do they quit buying? (What happened? How did we lose a customer?")

"Let me ask you this. How can we deliver to you, the salespeople, the right products, at the right time, with the right features, at the right price to give us competitive advantage if we can't answer these questions?"

- A Sales VP introducing CRM to the Sales Force

To illustrate just how critical "The 100% Solution" is, imagine a company attempting critical path financial planning and analysis but based upon incomplete and inaccurate accounting data—some in the computer, some on paper, and some residing only in people's heads. Why bother? Organizations successful in customer relationship management have created a foundation of complete and accurate sales data based upon 100% of the salespeople using CRM 100% of the time, with 100% quality information goal. In short, there is no difference between 0% and 99% of the sales force using CRM because either number is essentially worthless.

The 100% Solution is the only viable solution—and assuring that turns out to be the new task of field sales management.

100% Automation—The New Task for Sales Managers

So how is a sales manager supposed to do this? Become Big Brother? To enforce CRM use with "The Big Stick"?

"Oh great! Just what I really need, something else to do! I need to spend my time helping close business not enforcing some new system!"

Predictably (and perhaps fortunately) neither "Big Brother" or "Big Stick" works—and this manager is absolutely right. He or she doesn't need to spend valuable sales time enforcing some new corporate system. The key to making customer relationship management work—to actually achieving the 100% Solution—comes down to my First & Second Laws of Customer relationship management Success. These are the cornerstones around which successful implementations of CRM will be built:

The 1st Law: The direct benefits to sales managers, which have been too often overlooked, are as great or greater than to the salespeople.

The 2nd Law: Salespeople will invariably use automation as much and as well as they perceive their direct manager uses and depends on it.

So, what are the benefits to managers and how do management users create sales rep users?

The 1st Law: Management Rewards

Think about the job of a sales manager. When some years ago I was first promoted to branch sales manager I finally thought I had made it—until I discovered how little control I really had of what was going on in the field…and discovered "midnight madness".

"Midnight Madness"—"It's 12:00AM and I'm wide awake. The end of the month (quarter, year) is coming up and I'm having a midnight attack of the FUDS (fears, uncertainties, & doubts). Will we make the numbers?

How reliable is the forecast? Is there enough business in the pipeline? How confident do I feel?"

Now is when I realize how little control I really have as a manager over sales—certainly not like when I was a sales rep! I don't really have a lot of information about what's going on in the field and I worry about that.

"I'll call all my reps first thing in the morning and we'll go over each deal...again." (They'll appreciate that!)

Midnight Madness or "It's 12:00AM, You're Wide Awake!"

There are sales management questions that just have no good answers—the kind that wake you in the middle of the night...and keep you that way. Over two years, with more than 500 sales managers, we asked "The 12:00AM Question" to learn what are the key questions that managers need answers to and aren't getting—and that customer relationship management can provide through the 100% Solution. Here are a few...

"What's going on out there?"

Perhaps because most sales managers were first successful salespeople, they're used to being in control of events and staying on top of each sales situation. All that changes as a manager when you realize that the salespeople don't relish writing activity reports, educating you on each opportunity (especially daily), and answering "Did you..." questions ("Did you qualify that deal? Did you ask for the order?...). You want to find a way to know what's going on without "micromanaging"...and driving the sales people (and yourself) crazy.

"Where did all the leads go?"

Remember the 500 leads from that trade show? When you looked through the cards there were some great "Call me ASAP!" opportunities. You know (er...think) marketing send the leads to your sales reps. Now its been three months and it seems like nothing's happened. How? Didn't the reps follow up? (You told them to at your team meeting!) Nobody seems to be able to give you a real specific answer...black hole!

"What are the Reps up to?"

If the sales reps are in the office you know what they're doing, it just isn't selling. On the other hand when you haven't seen them for six weeks...well, you get a little nervous!

"Are we going to make the numbers?"

The big question. Will we make it? How accurate is the forecast? You're trying to remember every deal that should close. Even though the rep said "Not to worry" how confident do you really feel? The pressure's on from upstairs too!

"My best sales rep just quit!"

If you're really lucky he or she just retired to the Bahamas. If you're really unlucky, that rep now works for the competition and is coming after his or her old customers. To make it worse, the new salesperson you assigned says that she can't find any files to speak of and nobody seems to know what "Best Rep" was working on. Oh boy...

"How can I help?"

And here's the bottom-line, every manager's real question. You were probably a pretty good sales rep, even great! You love to sell, to make calls, to brainstorm and set strategies. Trouble is there's no time, the sales reps don't invite you on calls as much as you'd like, and when you do go you find its hard to really help "make it happen" because you're not as close to the account as the salesrep. (Another "schmooze" call). Rats...

Every manager tries to walk the line—between driving the salespeople crazy with reporting, business reviews, and "How's it going?" calls, and having enough information to do the real job of sales management: coaching, planning, and helping close business. Managers who have access to up-to-date sales progress data, as provided through CRM, spend less time asking "What's going on out there?" and more time doing their real job.

They can now stay in direct touch with every account and every opportunity progressing through the sales pipeline—and have the answers at hand to spell the end of "midnight madness" once and for all. Again, the First Law of Customer relationship management Success: The direct benefits to sales management are as great or greater than to the salespeople.

The 2nd Law: Salespeople will invariably use automation as much and as well as they perceive their direct manager uses and depends on it.

So how and why does a sales manager who is a strong user of CRM bring about 100% use and quality by the sales force? The answer is through a new management style: Fact-based Management

Fact-based management represents perhaps the most significant change in management technique of the last fifty years. At its maximum, it represents a total rethinking of manager's roles; at the minimum it is at least a significant change in the corporate and management culture.

Traditionally, sales managers have managed by "Feel". Managers have never had much in the way of direct information on accounts, sales progress, or the buying relationships established. What information that has been available has come from written call reports or manager/salesperson conversations—data often incomplete or inconsistent and difficult to consolidate or analyze to any great depth. Again, the manager is walking the line between getting enough information to manage well and using up rep's valuable selling time asking for written and oral reports. So a sales manager strives to get enough information to feel good about a deal or that the right things are being done in the field that will result in business—call this traditional "Feel-Based Management".

In Fact-Based Management, however, sales managers have direct access to all the "facts" about the progress of an account or sales opportunity combined with potentially an additional wealth of information from Corporate Information Systems and market data (from internal marketing,

Dun & Bradstreet market data, etc.). They are now able to essentially view these opportunities three ways:

1. Activity history—we can see what has already happened, good and bad, and understand how we got to where we are today.

2. Present Status—in the eyes of the salesperson, where do we stand today with this account or sales opportunity?

3. Future Plans—what does this salesperson plan to do next in order to advance this account towards the sale or goal? These come together in a typical fact-based coaching session:

A Fact-Based Coaching Session

Anne S., a sales representative for ABC Co. and her manager "meet" every Tuesday afternoon from 1:30PM to 2:00PM to review Anne's accounts and current sales opportunities. Anne works from her home office in St. Louis, phoning in to her manager, in New Hampshire. Both Anne and her manager share the customer relationship management database on their laptops and have her accounts displayed on the screen. They have both prepared for today's session by reviewing the top five accounts Anne has forecast to close this month.

$$* \qquad * \qquad * \qquad * \qquad *$$

Before ABC Co. introduced customer relationship management this was the typical conversation:

Manager: "Bring me up to date, Anne, on each of the deals you plan to close this month..."

Anne: "Okay. Well first there's XYX Co. and I feel good about this one. Remember how last week I was trying to get in to see the purchasing agent, well..." Anne begins the tedious process of educating her manager on the progress she has made.

Manager: "Why did you do that? Did you think about...? What are you going to do next?" And then on to the next deal...

Much of their half hour was spent bringing the manager up-to-date on what's happened during the last week—focusing on the past. Not only were her manager's "coaching" suggestions spur of the moment, Anne, like most salespeople, approached these sessions with a "Gotcha!" mentality—her manager was reviewing her performance looking for a "Gotcha!", i.e., correcting Anne for what she could have done better.

Today, with automation, that conversation—and results —have changed...

Manager: "Okay, Anne, let's look first at the account you have as the highest probability of closing for this month, XYC Co.. I can see here that your plan to get in and see the purchasing agent was successful and is says here that he sees no problems with cutting a P.O. by next week. Anything more you want to add...?"

Anne: "It was a good call. As I indicated, he does not meet with most vendors personally so I felt this was a good sign."

Manager: "Based on that, Anne, I tend to agree with you that this deal is an "A" account on the forecast. I've reviewed that you plan to meet this week with XYZ's president to wrap the deal and I think you have some good ideas. Let me give you some suggestions on how you may want to approach him..."

This was a true "Fact-Based" Coaching session, the intent to find ways to move the sale ahead, and focused on facts, not making management "feel" good about the progress of this sale. Anne and her manager have moved away from "Gotcha!" to "Mentor" management.

This session "worked" for both Anne and her manager because the customer sales progress information was accurate and up to date, allowing her manager to review the data before their meeting and formulate specific questions and ideas to help her advance the sale.

But what if Anne didn't want to use the system...or was busy and didn't have a chance to update the record fully (or at all) before the coaching session? That simply wouldn't have happened because Anne's manager relies on customer relationship management. For example…

Manager: "Okay, Anne, let's look first at the account you have as the highest probability of closing for this month, XYC Co.. I can see here that you were not able to get in and see the purchasing agent. That's too bad. Maybe you should…"

Anne: "No, I did get in and it was great. I just was a little busy and I didn't get around to putting it in the computer. Let me tell you all about it! I…"

Manager: "Excuse me, Anne. You're wasting our time. The purpose of our meeting is to plan together what to do next to close this deal, not to tell me what you've been doing. Besides that, Anne, I spent considerable time trying to develop some ideas to help you get in to see that purchasing agent and apparently that was another waste of my time…"

A clear example of "The Second Law of customer relationship management success: Salespeople will invariably use automation as much and as well as they perceive their direct manager uses and depends on it".

There are some important points to bring out from this hypothetical coaching session and what it really means to the changing job of sales management:

* Accountability—CRM creates a new accountability between salesperson and manager. Forecasts and action plans are based upon a wealth of facts as recorded by the salesperson, but the accuracy and value of forecasts and plans are only as good as the quality of the information in the system. A manager has a new accountability to the salesperson—to be well informed, to provide well thought out guidance—as well as greater accountability to corporate for greater forecast accuracy, more specific identification of opportunities and issues, and so forth.

* Management Preparation & Analytical Skills—Fact-based management enhances the role of sales managers as strategists and tacticians and lessens their role as "activity managers". Managers will spend more

time reviewing the status and development of sales opportunities, identifying successful and unsuccessful tactics, and conducting coaching sessions.

* "Mentor" Management & Coaching—In the selling process, managers will need to assume a new role as a "Mentor" than a "Gotcha!" manager. This will mean creating a new, often initially foreign, relationship with salespeople. Manager and salesperson must become a "strategic team", together applying their common skills and knowledge to advance and close the sale. By itself this will be one of the most difficult tasks for sales management—and necessary to eliminate the "Big Brother" mentality.

How do salespeople react to a fact-based management style? Greater accountability and management involvement may initially be viewed as taking away a sales rep's traditional independence. Salespeople, however, managed this way find they not only close more business (because they are receiving increased help and resources) but also that they actually empowered (and in some ways have increased independence) through less reporting and less time spent keeping their managers up-to-date. Salespeople who know what they are doing and are doing it well will probably receive less management attention than they do today—simply because they don't need it. It turns out that "Big Brother"—especially for top salespeople—is far more myth than reality.

Creating Mentor Management & Sales Acceptance

Becoming a mentor manager isn't always easy. It is not only a change in technique but also a change in the culture of the sales team. Here are some basic principle for mentor manager "wanna-be's":

* Don't confuse "Mentor" with "Buddy"—by definition, the role of a manager is somewhat authoritarian, responsible for returning goaled revenues to the corporation. For a mentor manager the best way to achieve this goal is to use his or her experience and skills to make salespeople

more successful—something now finally possible through the availability of better sales progress information. This means becoming a "best resource" not a "best friend".

* Glue your computer to your hip—Well, not literally; but in the 2nd Law we said that salespeople would use CRM as well as they perceived it was used by management. In short, it's not enough for a manager to use CRM for tracking, analysis, and planning behind closed doors (in the office, at home, etc.). The manager's laptop computer must become the "bible" of sales activity. It travels visibly with the manager at all times. Whenever an account is discussed, the manager refers to the system. During coaching sessions (especially face-to-face) the system is the primary discussion tool.

* Create the Sales "Team"—Through the enabling technology of CRM and the sharing of sales progress data, successful strategies and tactics can be shared among members of a sales unit—competitive intelligence, industry data, common large account information, etc.. The "mentor" relationship is not just between manager and salesperson but extends throughout the entire sales unit or organization.

* Visibly increase your personal "Q" Factor—"Q" is for "Quality". In a survey of salespeople regarding their opinion of their direct manager's quality, many responded that they felt managers were out of touch, didn't really know what was going on in the field, returned little value to the salesperson from the information and reports sent in, and that "times have changed since he or she was selling". In short, it's not enough for managers to simply have better information at hand; it has to be visibly and effectively used.

* Develop "Plans for Success" supported by facts—Salespeople want to feel that management has a plan for success; still many are skeptical of the "sales strategy of the week" that comes from "Corporate Disconnect", i.e., "Management doesn't really know what they're doing". Mentor managers are more successful and find greater sales

acceptance with the plans they develop simply because they are known to be based on comprehensive field data provided by the salespeople themselves.

* Complement & Counsel—A simple technique that is an essential tool of mentor managers. In the process of CRM coaching, it's all too easy to quickly find fault ("You should have done this or that!") and create an instantaneous "Big Brother" reaction. In the coaching process, find 2 or 3 things to "complement" a person on before "counseling" what might have been done better. For example: "Bob, this looks like an excellent new opportunity you've developed, and you've certainly qualified it well. What I am concerned about is…"

* Conduct "The Sales Team Strategy Session"—a fundamental technique for managers and salespeople which we'll discuss next in "The Four Step Process"..

The Four Step Process to "The 100% Solution"

In the beginning of every implementation of a customer relationship management system there are will be advocates ("Best idea we ever had!"), moderates ("I'll keep an open mind and I really hope it does work") and skeptics ("I'm not throwing my old system away but I'll try this if I have to…") We have already discussed why "selling" them on it or taking a "try it, you'll like it" approach won't work. So the question remains, "How do we initially create a 100% user base and build it to a 100% quality base?".

The most effective method is The Four Step Process—a series of evolutionary steps which has two objectives:

(1) move CRM from being a new (and perhaps initially somewhat uncomfortable) selling system to one which becomes a permanent part of the corporate culture.

(2) make CRM self-perpetuating in the long term, requiring minimal impetus from management for its effective use.

Not surprisingly however, it is management that is responsible for generating CRM's initial momentum.

The Four Step Process

STEP I: The Top Management Mandate

Critical to the long term success of a CRM project is to establish an initial base of 100% sales management and sales rep users—true whether automation is being rolled out to a pilot group or an entire sales force. In addition, we want to make it clear that CRM is not optional use—it is not on trial or test; it is now a permanent part of the corporate culture; there are large-scale corporate reasons that make this project essential to the company (see "Corporate Disconnect). This message absolutely must come from top corporate management not only because of its weight but also because a top management mandate empowers sales managers to require full CRM use by making it a part of their goals as well.

Certainly this kind of mandate will not produce the level of quality users needed, but it does create a starting point for developing a more complete corporate sales database and from which the customer relationship management system can be further tuned and refined.

STEP II. The Sales Team Strategy Session

At the same time as we are mandating automation, we would like to begin developing some sense of system ownership by the sales force—especially because we want our tuning and refining efforts to reflect the needs and wants of sales as much as possible. The Sales Team Strategy Session begins this process plus requires a visible commitment by salespeople to make the CRM project successful.

The Sales Team Strategy Session may be conducted at any time but is perhaps most effective in conjunction with initial roll out or user training. Led by the unit sales manager, the session is attended by direct report salespeople and other cross-functional personnel who may have an interest or eventual role in the project, with the exception of senior management who should not attend at this point.

The steps and elements of the session are as follows:

1.) Company Values: Setting the Stage—Restatement by manager of the corporate mandate and reasons why the CRM project is critical to the success of the entire company. "CRM is not an option. Our purpose today is, as a team, determine how to make this new system work for us! The company is committed to the success of this project and I have personally committed us to its success!"

2.) Identify Sales Unit's Challenges in the Marketplace—In an interactive team session identify the major challenges this specific sales team faces in its marketplace, i.e. competitive intrusion, leads, geographic constraints, customer satisfaction…

3.) Identify Hi-Value Automation Solutions—apply the characteristics of the CRM system that will address the identified unit challenges.

4.) Identify Sales Manager's Needs & Challenges —For example, requirement to improve forecast accuracy, obtain and effectively apply available resources, strategic planning, etc. Identify CRM characteristics that address these as well. "As a team (manager and salespeople) we have both unique and common goals which we must address working together and towards which customer relationship management can be of value."

5.) Establish Team Rules & Tasks—As a team, establish and agree upon the functional rules and tasks to make CRM successful in the unit, e.g., everyone will use CRM, weekly coaching session times and data requirements established, incentives and/or consequences defined.

6.) Statement of Position—the most important element of the team strategy session, the sales unit creates a unit statement of position which using the first five elements details how this unit has committed to make CRM successful within itself. At the conclusion of this, the team makes a formal stand-up presentation to a senior sales or corporate manager or creates a document for submission.

The fundamental results of the Sales Team Strategy Session are that team interdependencies are already being formed, management's requirements are clearly understood, team members have had a role in determining how to best utilize CRM, and, most importantly, the team has delivered a public commitment to success. At this point, we have provided a sales manager a foundation from which to work.

STEP III: The Manager-Dependent System

Once a 100% user base has been established and the team strategy session completed, the job of building quality begins, specifically improving the quantity and quality of data being entered by the sales representatives. This task falls to the first-line sales managers and will be the direct result of managers utilizing fact-based management techniques. In short, the level of quality and completeness the manager requires in order to better do his or her job of managing will determine the quality level of the users.

Users who have been moderates or skeptics will only begin to perceive the value of an CRM system through using it at a high data quality level.

IV. The Peer-Managed System

As we discussed earlier, one of management's automation tasks will be to develop a team environment and mutual sharing of critical sales information (large account team selling, competitive intelligence, lead distribution, industry data, and so forth). In some cases, teams may also include service and customer support field personnel who need to share and exchange account information with sales. As the team environment is built over time, interdependencies among team members are created...like the sales manager, members count on the completeness and accuracy of CRM information in order to do their jobs. In short the use and quality of CRM is mandated and managed by peers, not only management.

Peer-managed systems are not built overnight and are the result of long-term corporate and sales management commitment. They are, however, virtually self-perpetuating, can be considered to have become then a permanent part of the corporate culture, and represent the critical goal of customer relationship management.

So Who "Sells" the Sales Managers on CRM?

It becomes clear that if the sales managers are key to the success, we're going to have to "sell" them on CRM. Fortunately, many of the same techniques we developed to use with the salespeople also apply:

* The Top Management Mandate sets the stage for the managers as well.

* A Management Team Strategy Session precedes the Sales Team Strategy Sessions with much the same agenda and conducted by senior sales management.

* Senior Management-Dependent Systems—Upper sales management levels utilize CRM as a fact-based tool to manage their manager-level reports.

* Peer-Managed Management Systems—development of interdependent management teams sharing common market information.

* Specialized Management Education—one of the most fundamental and large-scale tasks will be educating managers not only how to operate an CRM system but how to apply it as a management analysis and coaching tool.

Putting It All Together—Integrating CRM Capacity and Capability

In corporate's quest to design and implement customer relationship management, and with the increasing capabilities of computer hardware and software, we have entered a new world of sales and marketing in which the level of what is theoretically possible has reached undreamed of heights. Unfortunately the level of business skill development to enable managers and salespeople to achieve these results has lagged far behind the ability of corporate information systems to provide technology.

The message then is this. In the world of customer relationship management, there is today the capacity, provided by technology, to create automation systems that positively impact productivity and effectiveness throughout the corporation. It is often ignored, however, that this technology is people-driven, that is, it relies upon the user's capability to apply it in order to achieve optimum results. Small wonder, then, that CRM sometimes meets with user resistance, i.e., users who feel more confident in their capability to apply older, though less efficient manual systems.

We need then to view the investment in customer relationship management as two discreet elements. First, the costs of Capacity—purchasing hardware and automation software, systems design, and user operations training—are basic elements of most project plans and well understood. To this we need to add the less well defined but critically necessary investment of Capability to assure results through specialized management and sales skill training that integrates automation technology.

In summary then, Customer relationship management's Big Payoff will be found in management's new capability to direct the path of business based more on fact than feel. This capability, however, will be based on three factors: (1) the accuracy and completeness of the information collected by the sales force (and like any other business system, anything less than 100% in unacceptable), (2) the business analysis and performance management skills of sales managers, and (3) management motivation of the salespeople to make maximum use of CRM.

Achieving this is the critical new task of field sales management—a task that can only become reality when sales managers become the true power users of customer relationship management.

HAPPY CUSTOMERS—LOOKING "DOWN" THE "UP" STAIRCASE

Happy customers...everyone wants them. They're certainly preferable to unhappy customers, or even marginally satisfied. It has been said that "happy customers are the engine that grows a business". If that's true then finding a way to consistently create them should (and usually is) a primary goal of any growing business. But while the goal may be clear, just how to accomplish "customer happiness" is often less so.

The usual approach is to create some sort of Customer Satisfaction Program. Perhaps we'll call on the customer more frequently or offer a convenient "hot line" for quick resolution of problems or complaints. Maybe we'll hire a customer satisfaction representative to let our customers know how much we really care. We might create a "loyal customer rewards" program offering special pricing, incentives, or rewards to our good customers...and let's not forget customer entertainment! Finally, of course, we'll train all out people in customer relations and the importance of satisfied and happy customers. And when all is said and done our customers are usually not that much "happier" than when we started! What went wrong?

Customer satisfaction tends to depend upon The Four "P's": Product, Pricing, Programs, and People. Chances are, however, that if your customers are not as "happy" as you would like them to be, the problem isn't with the first three...it's with your People!

For better or worse, our customers tend to define their relationship with us—and to a large extent measure their overall satisfaction with our product or services—in terms of their relationship with the people they interact with from our company. Invariably, customers accurately sense whether someone is truly interested in them and their needs or whether that person is just "going through the motions". Unfortunately, no amount of customer relations training will turn an employee who really doesn't care about the customer into one who does. Recently, a director of customer service, faced with just this problem, said to me, "I guess we have been hiring the wrong people!"…but was he right?

The fact is that the culture of our companies creates the attitudes of our people towards our customers, a model we call The Corporate Staircase. Our ability as an organisation to produce happy customers really depends upon our overall company culture–the attitudes, beliefs, motivations, and management style–of your company far more than your ability to hire the "right" people.

Think of your company organisation as a staircase. Standing on the top is corporate management. Middle managers and field managers fill the next lower steps. They are followed by your customer representatives including sales, service, or anyone who "touches" the customer. On the bottom steps stand our customers. The critical question is "Which way are your people facing .. Up or Down the Staircase?"

In many companies, everyone other than the customers is facing upwards. In other words, our employees are most concerned with what the people above them think, i.e. producing Happy Superiors. The satisfaction or approval of their superiors is of primary importance, determines their income and potential to climb further up the staircase, and defines their attitudes and behaviors. In this model, an employee's superior is the Customer!…and it is quite probable that employees do an outstanding job of assuring this "customer" is fully satisfied! In an "Up Staircase Company" it's not unusual to hear comments such as "Our customers (the ones who actually buy our product or service) are just never satisfied! All they want is a lower price and more, more, more! They don't appreciate all we do for them! They make me look bad! They're a pain…"

In other companies, everyone is facing down the staircase, ultimately towards that most important, end-user customer. But a "Down Staircase Company" has gone a step further: it has redefined the meaning of the word "customer". In this company, each "step" views the step immediately below as a "customer". In other words, top management believes its most important task is assuring the success of their customer: the managers who report to them (a successful employee being a "happy customer"). Middle managers and field managers believe that their job is to assure the success of their customer, i.e., the people who report to them (the representatives who "touch" the customer). Success, then, for any customer representative is clearly defined as assuring the Success of the true customer, not simply pleasing management! To look at it another way, my success is always measured by the success of my "customer" wherever I stand on the company "staircase".

In our Down Staircase Company the equation is clear: Happy Staff = Happy Customers! Any employee who lives in a corporate culture of "customer success and who believes the company is honestly interested in his/her success will bring that same attitude to dealing with his or her customers. Perhaps the critical question, however, is "Can an Up Staircase Company ever produce truly 'happy' customers?"

Happy Customers…creating them is a matter of capacity and capability. Perhaps before we add more capacity (programs, incentives, personnel) we need to take a close look at whether we have the organisational capability to produce truly happy customers. Which way are your people facing on the Staircase?

THE QUEST FOR MARKET LEADERSHIP

Market Leadership or Leadership. It is the often unstated but very real goal of every business. For many companies, however, it is more a dream than an achievable reality. Nonetheless, today's marketplace is full of opportunity for companies with the vision, drive, and knowledge to become market leaders.

"Market Leadership" might be thought of as an organisation attaining the majority share of the available market for their products or services and establishing an unassailable, long-term competitive position. The definition may be straightforward but the "how to" is somewhat less so. After all, achieving market leadership will mean unseating the current market leader (which may be a much larger company with greater resources). It means winning new customers by taking "satisfied" customers away from the competition! It will require a focused effort by the company with a high degree of risk! No wonder many organisations think twice before launching a concerted drive to become the market leader.

Is the key to market leadership found in new product innovation? Added-value selling? Superior customer service? Aggressive pricing? Intensive marketing? Improved sales skills? Expanded manufacturing/distribution capacity? New technologies such as customer relationship management or the internet? The answer is "all of these...and much more". By itself, any one of these—new products, added-value selling, customer service, pricing, marketing, skills, capacity, and technology—can produce a sales benefit and a competitive edge (at least until it is equaled or surpassed by a competitor). Market leadership requires all of these and one more...a Victory of Strategy.

136

The Rule of Market Leadership

To dominate a market, you must dominate every sales territory or market area. To dominate a territory you must dominate the key accounts (customers) within it. To dominate the key accounts, you must win the majority of the sales opportunities in each account. To dominate the opportunities you must dominate the contact relationships, i.e., individual contacts who make or influence each sales decision…and to lose one is to lose all.

Strategy Tools:

Market leadership requires a new set of sales tools. In order of importance, the first is "Strategy Tools".

As "The Rule of Market Leadership" suggests, it requires an increasingly complex set of strategies and tactics to win each of the contact relationships, opportunities, accounts, and territories that make up a company's market. For example, winning a complex sales opportunity (multiple contacts, long and complex decision cycle, etc.) requires a different set of strategies and sales tactics than "winning" an individual contact relationship. Winning a key account requires a salesperson to win all contacts plus win all account opportunities plus develop a plan to develop and protect the account…and so forth.

Salespeople, for the most part, have been poorly equipped to plan and manage more than their contacts. Traditionally many sales organisations have focused only on building relationships with contacts, assuming that "winning" at this level was enough, i.e. if you won the contacts, the opportunities, accounts, and the territory must follow by default. Unfortunately it doesn't work out that way.

A market leadership strategy—from territory to contact—requires a new focus by the entire sales organisation, and a set of integrated business planning tools…or processes…to help salespeople manage the added complexity of opportunities, key accounts, and territories.

Technology Tools

Unlike the past, today's salespeople rarely work in a vacuum. Not only must salespeople often work effectively with other parts of the organisation (sales teams, management, service, support, manufacturing, finance, etc.), their ability to execute their strategies increasingly depends on coordinating and communicating their strategies and customer data to each of them.

The ultimate value of customer relationship management (CRM) technology is not in the "sales productivity tools" it contains, such as calendar, "to do" management, etc. CRM's greatest value is as a strategic planning tool and a company-wide communications infrastructure.

To begin with, the sales planning and analysis processes for contact, opportunity, account, and territory management should be built directly into CRM software. This allows for easy updating of plans throughout the year—and the ability to electronically share real-time plan and sales progress data with sales team members, sales management, marketing, and others who can benefit from "live" customer information.

Other CRM sales tools such as product configurators can help salespeople quote and price products more rapidly than ever before—and may even provide specific value and convenience to the customer. Again, however, their greatest value may be in increased configuration accuracy with immediate communications to order entry and manufacturing or distribution—resulting in increased customer satisfaction.

Technology further provides the company (and salesperson) improved ways to communicate directly with the customer. Marketing encyclopedias can deliver extremely detailed and accurate product data via a variety of media and communications technologies. Even "simple" tools such as electronic mail, web sites, and fax enhance customer communications.

Technology tools can link the customer to the company through the salesperson or directly through on-line computer capabilities such as the internet or intranets. In either case, both company and customer can mutually provide and share information critical to the success and satisfaction of both.

Putting It All Together

We began with the question: "Is the key to market leadership found in new product innovation? Added-value selling? Superior customer service? Aggressive pricing? Intensive marketing? Improved sales skills? Expanded manufacturing/distribution capacity? New technologies such as customer relationship management or the internet?" The answer was: "All of these...and more". A company's potential to excel in each of these areas—and potential for market leadership—can be viewed in terms of its strategic and its technology tools.

New product innovation can create market position but only if the new product is one which will create customer demand. Using technology can enable a product planning group to more accurately assess customer needs and new product response.

Added-Value Selling strategies depend on an understanding of what represents real value to a customer. "Live" customer data combined with "strategic account, opportunity, and contact profiling can enable the sales organization to develop and deliver "on-target" added-value programs.

Superior customer service depends on customer knowledge by "everyone who touches the customer". Customer information and business plans, provided through technology tools, enables the development of focused offerings with more "personalized" customer service.

Aggressive pricing can be an effective sales tool when used to attain a defined market goal and based on the availability of the comprehensive, accurate market knowledge that technology and strategy tools can provide.

Marketing programs are only as good as their focus. Are they targeted at the right buyers, with the right message, at the right time? The solution: again, comprehensive, accurate market knowledge that technology and strategy tools can provide.

The ability of manufacturing/distribution to correctly anticipate demand is critical to any organisation's success. Connecting these groups directly to the sales "pipeline"—current sales opportunities—allows them to track progress and more accurately adjust long term capacity and inventory planning.

And Sales Skills…salespeople who are "armed" with better customer and prospect information and comprehensive planning processes increase their capability to make better sales decisions, i.e. execute the right sales tactic, the to right contact, with the right message, at the right time, to achieve optimum results.

In Summary

Achieving market leadership is, of course, more than just implementing strategy and technology tools. It depends upon people—people in every area of the company who are motivated, willing, and capable of doing their jobs in a superior manner. This may be the greatest challenge of all. We do know one thing for sure, however. Our people will never do their jobs in a manner than enables us to create market leadership if we fail to provide them with the necessary tools.

CUSTOMER RELATIONSHIP MANAGEMENT AN OPPORTUNITY FOR COMPETITIVE ADVANTAGE?

Customer Relationship Management…it seems there is a new business "buzz word" every year. This year it's "Customer Relationship Management" or "CRM". Not long ago it was Partnering. Added-Value is still around as well. Actually CRM is a pretty good catch phrase simply because there is nothing more important than the relationships we establish and maintain with our customers.

I spoke at a recent sales conference and asked my audience, "How many of you think that customer relationship management is important?". Not surprisingly, every head nodded and every hand went up. Then I asked, "How many of you have a clear strategy in your company for customer relationship management?". Many, but not all, hands again were raised. Finally I asked, "How many of you think that your CRM strategy is being well executed and is making a measurable difference?". Now only a few hands could be seen, half-raised, among the crowd.

There's the problem. We all embrace CRM as a good idea but when it comes to developing a customer relationship strategy and then executing it…well, we're a bit less confident. We shouldn't feel that way about something as critical to the success of our businesses as CRM.

There are two fundamental questions you must ask–and successfully answer–if you want to develop a customer relationship management strategy, i.e., one that helps you gain new customers, maximize the potential of current customers, and protect your most important customers from competitive intrusion: What kind of relationship do you want to establish with your customer? And What must you do to create and maintain that relationship?

What kind of relationship do you want to establish with your customer?

When we think about relationships, many of us–and most salespeople–think of the personal one-on-one relationships we establish with key customer personnel. Without question, personal relationships are important. The axiom "People buy from people they like" is still true. The problem is that people come and go in the business world, both in the customer's company and in our own. So, as useful as personal relationships may be, they're dangerous to depend on for long term success.

The real question is What kind of relationship do you want your Company to establish with your customers?

- Your customers will directly or indirectly interact with many different people in your company across the enterprise, not just your sales representatives. How do you want your customer to feel about his or her overall interaction with your company? What do you want your customer's to value about you as a result?

- What are the Key Values you bring your customers; that is, what are the reasons your customers should only want to buy from you? Your key value(s) should form the basis of the customer relationship you want to create. Can you clearly and succinctly define and communicate your key values?

- Are your Key Values unique and important enough to your customers that if they fully understood and appreciated them they would clearly prefer you over your competitors? Take a few moments before you answer this question and take a hard look. Remember that you simply cannot build a powerful business relationship if you can't offer something the customer needs and values better than your competition. You may need to rethink your key values.

- Does the customer's every interaction with your entire company support, sell, and enhance this key value message? Does each interaction enhance and build the relationship?

Let's look at the mythical ABC Company. ABC believes its key values are the quality of its products and the responsiveness of its people. ABC must first ask itself if its customers feel these key values are important—important enough to establish an exclusive business relationship with ABC. ABC must then ask itself if its quality and responsiveness are unique enough to base its customer relationships upon. If the answer to both questions is "Yes", they must then ask whether every customer interaction—with sales, service, billing, delivery, etc.—actively supports the messages of quality and responsiveness. Finally, does the customer consistently feel that their relationship with the company as a whole is so strong that it can easily survive any change in ABC's personnel?

What must we do to create and maintain that relationship

Step 1: Definition & Action Plans

Creating and managing the customer relationship is clearly an enterprise-wide task. The company as a whole must define—and clearly communicate to every employee—what it wants to be the basis of the customer relationship (key values). Each function of the company must clearly define:

(1) how it contributes and impacts (positively or negatively) the customer relationship,

(2) develop a specific action plan of what it can do to provide a greater contribution, and

(3) how it depends upon and needs to interact better with other functions.

Step 2: Customer Communication & Internal Change

If there is a "single point of failure" in CRM, this is it! Too many companies do a good job of defining why customers should buy from them (other than just product or price) but seem to forget to tell the customer! In other words, we create a potentially powerful message that could help build stronger customer relationships but fail to clearly establish it in the mind of the customer. So in the final analysis it's still business as usual.

It is an important consideration that unless your company's customer relationships are already exactly as you want them, you will have to do something different than you are today. Different results are the result of different actions. This means that everyone in your company—and especially the sales force—will have to do some things differently than in the past. As the prime point of customer contact—and as the people who set the direction of the customer relationship—this directly impacts your sales organization.

Look again at ABC Company. They did a fine job defining their key values upon which to base the customer relationship. They determined what each job function and each employee needed to do and they communicated it well to their organization. New marketing and advertising focused on the unique value ABC offered. Unfortunately nothing really changed—sales and win/loss ratios stayed the same and the company won and lost the same number of new and old customers as the year before. Clearly customer relationships were not strengthened or enhanced. What went wrong?

The problem was ABC's sales force. It wasn't that they weren't good salespeople. The problem is they were excellent salespeople! In fact, they were so good that they were not about to change what had worked for them in the past. Their "sales pitch" stayed the same and they continued "building" the customer relationship one-on-one, not "company-to-company". To a lesser degree the same was true with employees in other job functions; they continued to do their jobs they way they always had with lip service to the company's CRM initiatives.

Step 3: Managing the Initiatives as a New Product

So in the end it's all about execution. Companies successful in Customer Relationship Management have learned that results happen when employees actively embrace new initiatives (much like they would an exciting new product) and carry out the prescribed action plan (to sell it).

In other words, try viewing and positioning your Customer Relationship Management initiative as a true product, the cost to the customer of which is embedded in the price of the "standard" products you sell. After all, your CRM program is designed to first benefit your customer and through them your company. It is the responsibility of every employee to both "sell" and "deliver" the CRM product successfully to the customer.

Package your CRM program as you would a product, supported with marketing collateral, support, and a strong selling strategy. Put the same effort and enthusiasm into teaching your sales force your CRM product and how to sell it as you do teaching them to sell any new product.

Make sure that managers in all functions clearly understand the initiatives and action plans and how each employee is expected to perform. Assure that each manager understands that it is his or her responsibility to manage their business as expected.

Finally create a series of metrics or measurements of how you will measure the success of CRM—and tie an element of employee compensation (sales, managers, and others) to achieving those metrics. Aggressively track and measure. Make CRM your most powerful tool for real and new competitive advantage!

DEATH OF A SALESMAN?

Willy Loman didn't have one. He couldn't even have imagined one. Even if he could have imagined one he wouldn't have been able to see why he would need one.

"Willy", of course, is playwright Arthur Miller's most famous character from *Death of a Salesman*. He was the master salesman of the 1950's who in Miller's play is told that what he's done successfully for so many years just doesn't work anymore...that times and the world around him changed but he hasn't. His company simply doesn't need him anymore! For Willy, selling was straightforward. It was traveling the territory, making calls on customers and prospects, "detailing" the product, building one-to-one customer relationships, and using his well-honed sales skills. What Willy couldn't have imagined was the computer as an essential sales tool, much less the Internet, electronic mail, sales force automation, and on and on and on.

Willy might have asked, *"Why do I need all this technology? It's just taking time away from the real business of selling: face-to-face time with the customer!"*

As sales organisations and their corporations make ever larger investments in these new technologies, the question surfaces, "Do salespeople really need all this technology?". Do we all need to become computer users? Does today's sales rep need to acquire and master a new range of skills apart from selling? The simple answer is a resounding "Yes!"

Willy: *"It seems to me that these companies have just fallen in love with these new technology toys and don't really know much about selling. My customers don't care about whether or not I have a computer!"*

Willy is partially right; his customers don't care whether or not he has a *computer.* Customer expectations of their salespeople are changing, however. Today's customer increasingly expects his or her sales representative to:

- be better informed;
- to have virtually instant information to accurate and up-to-date pricing and product information;
- to respond quicker to customer requests, questions, and issues;
- to produce and deliver proposals and other written communications faster and error-free;
- to have a better knowledge of competition,
- to know more about the customer's company.
- To make more effective and productive use of the customer's time

A salesperson's ability–or inability–to meet these expectations becomes as much a part of his or her *competitive advantage* as product or price. Today's "technology toys" are specifically designed to provide salespeople with exactly these capabilities.

As far as *face-to-face time*, the "new technologies of selling" are designed to make that time more productive and more effective. How much time did Willy spend gathering needed information (if he could get it) on a customer or prospect, or to prepare for a sales call? How many times did he say to a customer, "I'll get back to you with that information" because he didn't have it readily available–and have to make a second sales call instead of one? Most importantly, how would he have fared against more efficient, productive, and *effective* competitors?

Willy's customers are not the only ones who are changing. So is his company. Customer expectations extend not only to the salesperson, they include his or her company as well. Many companies have traditionally operated more like a group of smaller companies who needed to work together but didn't very well. Those *small companies* were called *sales, customer service, marketing, finance, manufacturing, operations, administration* and so on.

Willy: *"That's true. I've had customers ask me* 'Don't your departments ever talk to one another?' *I've lost customers because I was the only one who* *seemed to understand their needs . I always wondered why the company couldn't fix that problem."*

There was a pretty good reason why that "problem" couldn't be fixed: *communications.* Before computer systems became common in business (the "Paper Age") it was virtually impossible to collect, collate, and share (i.e., communicate) accurate and real-time customer information across the business enterprise— to everyone who *touched* the customer. Until the fairly recent advent of personal computers and networks, computer systems were only used for scientific applications or to process accounting or financial data and track manufacturing and distribution–and even then it was difficult to get information to those who really needed it. Until salespeople could be provided with portable notebook computers and powerful data communications capabilities, few companies had real-time, accurate information on their customers or could communicate needed information directly to the sales force.

One of the most important corporate changes of the last ten years is the *Enterprise Concept,* and it was brought about entirely by the new technologies. Under the Enterprise Concept, each and every area or function of a company is dependent on and works hand-in-hand with every other function *across the business enterprise.* Each contributes and shares a corporate *Knowledge Base* (using advanced database technology and data communications) for improved decision-making and to better meet customer needs. The investment value is clear even though the technology costs and implementation challenges are great. The greatest challenge to implementing the *Enterprise Concept,* however, has been changing the way people throughout the company view their jobs. No longer can an employee be just a part of the sales department or marketing, service, finance, and so forth.

Willy: *"It sounds like you're trying to tell me that there's more to my job than* Selling*".*

Ultimately we are all now in the "sales department". Every employee in every function potentially makes a contribution that impacts our ability as a company to sell our product and meet customer needs. Salespeople are unique–they are the only people in the entire company who really "know" the customer–his/her needs, goals, business issues, satisfaction, likes and dislikes. There is no information more vital to the success of the company and it can only come from one source: field sales. When an organisation is successful with the *Enterprise Concept* and armed with better customer and market information, it is able to *produce the right products, at the right time, marketed and priced in the right way, to the right customers to produce competitive advantage for its sales force.* And that's what "selling" is all about!

Willy: *"Well, I see what you're saying. Still, I just don't like computers. All this Windows stuff confuses me. I guess I'm just an old dog who can't learn a new trick."*

If only there was an easy answer to this! Too many salespeople–and sales managers–continue to be needlessly concerned over whether they can learn to use today's computers and software. Without exception, the answer is again "Yes they can!", with the caveat "but it may take some time and practice and a little frustration from time to time". Many new computer users fear breaking the computer, erasing all those bits and bytes of data, or being asked to learn a programming language. It's important to understand that, unlike the "computer systems" many of us began with even 15 or 20 years ago, computers and their "application software" are increasingly easy to use and understand (even though they occasionally still do "strange" things for which there appears to be no reasonable explanation). No business user will be asked to "program" and, following simple procedures, it is unlikely that a user will ever *permanently* "wipe out" all the data he or she has entered or "break" the computer.

Salespeople are not the only professionals who have felt–and had to adapt–to the demands of technology. Up until the mid-1970's, many accountants still utilized manual ledgers for company bookkeeping; manufacturing managers had to learn state-of–the-art systems for capacity planning and inventory management; and on and on.

At the same time that some of us are busy "adapting" , an entirely new breed of salesperson has been emerging over the last 10 years from today's schools and universities. He or she is more than computer literate–they are *computer adept*. They already have years of hands-on experience in computer systems and fundamental Office applications such as word processing and spreadsheets. They are proficient at "surfing" the Internet and researching information, and especially strong in the use of new communications tools such as electronic mail and network conferencing. As they seek professional employment, they view these technology tools as *necessities* not "nice to haves". More and more companies are finding that their ability to attract and keep top sales talent relies, in part, on staying on the leading edge of selling and corporate technology.

Willy: *"That's true. In my company we hired a new marketing manager six months ago. He quit recently and said it was because he couldn't do his job here–that he couldn't get the information he needed because we didn't have a good marketing database. At the time I thought that was fine; get rid of another computer guy. Now I'm not so sure…"*

The bottom line simply is this: the business of selling–for better or worse and even if we might prefer it otherwise–has changed, is changing, and will continue to change. Technology and changing customer expectations are at the very root of this change and both will continue to set its future direction. The challenge for today's professional salesperson is more than just to *adapt* to the new technologies; it is to *master* them and learn how to *leverage* them as powerful tools to create new sources of selling advantage.

Even Willy might have agreed…

PART VII

ON SUCCESS...THE SUCCESS TRAPS:
The 7 Fatal Traps On The Journey to Success

THE SUCCESS TRAPS

What is Success?

It's such a great question because there's no great answer! Success, I suppose, is *what you make it!* It's whatever you decide it is. It's personal, for you, and no one else.

Success is a stretch. It's usually about accomplishing something that is important to you that makes your life better. Success can be about family or work or something very personal. It can be about your achievements in business, sport, academics, or a thousand other things. For many of us, it's about Sales! No matter what, it's always about reaching a bit higher, about being the very best you can be.

Recently an interviewer asked me, "Do you consider yourself successful?"

"Yes, I think so", I answered. And then I added, "But not as successful as I'm working on!"

"Well then," he smiled, "What advice would you give people about how they can become more successful?"

"Actually," I answered, "I'm not sure there's any advice I could give anyone about how to become more successful. Success is a pretty personal thing and it's different for everyone. Maybe I could tell them how to do what I've done but I'm not sure that's especially helpful."

*"Well, what **can** you say about Success?" asked the interviewer.*

I thought about it for a few minutes. "Achieving success is really pretty easy—if you can just avoid falling in the Traps along the way!"

"Really? Tell us more…"

I've gotten most everything I've ever dreamed of and a good bit more. Some days even I'm surprised. When I'm asked I usually attribute my good fortune to having had a lot of really good luck. But fortunately or unfortunately I have family and good friends who will correct me in front of people. *"Don't listen to him. Any "luck" he had he made!"* I suppose…

I spent over twenty years in sales and management with great companies: IBM, Digital Equipment, Dun+Bradstreet, and Source Services. I did very well. Not screamingly well but there were moments, a few flashes of brilliance. And I learned a lot. Mostly I just learned how to avoid the Seven Fatal Traps on the Journey to Success!

But that's not where the story begins. It all starts in June of 1995 on a beach…(and if you're going to start a success story, where better than a beach, I ask you?).

BEGINNINGS

Dorado Beach, Puerto Rico–

Sue and I and the kids arrived in sunny Puerto Rico on a beautiful, hot June day ready for two great weeks of sun, surf, and just perhaps the occasional margarita (Sue and I, not the kids). We had a great "casita" that opened right on to the beach under crystal clear Caribbean skies. The perfect vacation ahead.

When I left on Friday, the president of my employer, Sales Technologies (a Dun+Bradstreet company), asked me if I would mind calling in on Monday morning.

"I'm really sorry to ask you to do this on your vacation but we're making some important announcements that morning that I know you'll want to hear."

"Couldn't you just tell me now?" I asked.

"Sorry, can't say a thing until the official announcement! Why don't you call in after lunch?"

Things had been going pretty well at Sales Technologies and D+B was a pretty good parent company. I suspected that we would announce expansion plans, maybe into Europe, or something similar. Whatever the announcement was going to be, I hoped it might offer some good opportunity.

Early Monday afternoon, I forced myself up from my beach lounger, picked up my margarita and headed for the telephone by the poolside bar. A half hour later I was back on the beach.

"So, what's the big news?" asked my wife.

"Oh," I said, *"They just wanted to announce that they were closing the company. The good news is that we get three weeks severance."*

One of Sue's greatest strengths is her practicality. *"Well, in that case, I guess we better pack up and see about getting a flight home so you can get busy and find another job."* Sue, of course, knew without looking that we had four children and less than $5,000 in the bank.

"No, let's don't," I said.*" I was thinking about it on the way back to the beach (a journey of at least 3 to 4 minutes). I think we're all set. Why don't we just go in business for ourselves?"*

"Doing what?" Sue asked.

"Well," I answered, *"I'm not exactly sure yet but I figure we've got two weeks to figure it out…and the best part is that you're here with the president of the company! Do you want another margarita?"*

"Two, please"

*   *   *

There are people who have said I was very brave, that they would never have the "courage" to do what I did. There are people who have said that I was crazy (just because I had 4 kids, no cash, no customers, and no plan!). In retrospect, I tend to agree with the latter. I like to think of it as a period of extended temporary insanity and divine intervention. Consider what happened…

Shortly before we returned home I had decided on developing a sales consulting and motivational speaking business. I made a few calls to just a few friends just before we left.

The day we returned home a message was waiting on the answering machine from someone at IBM. *"Tim, we wondered if you were free tomorrow to come down to New York and consult with us on a new sales offering we're considering. We can pay you $5,000 and expenses…*

A call from Apple Computer: *"Tim, would you be interested in speaking at a series of sales conferences we're planning. In addition to your speaking fee, we'd like you to have a new Powerbook laptop to use".*

A call from US West Direct: *"Tim, we looking for a speaker for our sales conference and…"*

By Christmas, after just five months in business, we had made a *profit* of over $70,000.

Oh, did I mention that during this time of insanity and divine intervention I was working on a very simple rule of success? *If they don't know about you, they can't buy from you!*

Along with piles of faxes, hundreds of phone calls and emails, I managed to write and publish my first book, write four articles for major sales and marketing magazines, gain a publisher for a second book, and secure a contract to write a bi-weekly column for a national sales newsletter. I wanted to make sure that people noticed me!

Sounds like a lot of hard work, doesn't it? Well, absolute terror will do that to you! The truth is, however, that although it was a *lot* of *difficult* work it wasn't *hard work*–at least not in the sense of not being fun. I loved every moment of it–and still do!

And we just keep on growing…

It sounds almost too good to be true, doesn't it. I feel that way myself sometimes. But it almost didn't turn out this way. There were so many times when I could have easily given up and started looking for another job.

I could have fallen in *The Success Traps*. Each one of them guaranteed to trip up all my success plans and efforts. And they're sneaky–they can snag you before you even know it! Avoiding the success traps had more to do with my eventual success than anything I ever did to find business! And I still have to work to avoid them every day…

This isn't about how to start your own business (although if you're thinking about doing so it's not a bad place to start!). This is just a book about Success–however you define it—in sales, or in the company you work for, in sports, in your family and your friends, in your life!

If you're motivated to find your own success–and, as the golfers say, you can stay "out of the traps"–you're going to make it!

The Success Trap #1:

"AS GOD IS MY WITNESS, I THOUGHT TURKEYS COULD FLY"

* * * * *

Les: It's a helicopter, and it's coming this way. It's flying something behind it, I can't quite make it out, it's a large banner and it says, uh–Happy…Thaaaaanksss…giving!…From…W…...K…...R…...P!!

Les: No parachutes yet. Can't be skydivers…I can't tell just yet what they are, but–Oh my God, Johnny, they're turkeys!! Johnny, can you get this? Oh, they're plunging to the earth right in front of our eyes! One just went through the windshield of a parked car! Oh, the humanity! The turkeys are hitting the ground like sacks of wet cement! Not since the Hindenberg tragedy has there been anything like this!

Johnny: Les? Are you there? Les isn't there. (composing himself) Thanks for that on-the-spot report, Les, and for those of you who just tuned in, the Pinedale Shopping Mall has just been bombed with live turkeys. Film at eleven.

Venus: Les! Are you okay?

Les: I don't know. A man and his two children tried to kill me. After the turkeys hit the pavement, the crowd kind of scattered, but some of them tried to attack *me!* I had to jam myself into a phone booth! Then Mr. Carlson had the helicopter land in the middle of the parking lot. I guess he thought he could save the day by turning the rest of the turkeys loose. It gets pretty strange after that.

Andy: Les, c'mon now, tell us the rest.

Les: I really don't know how to describe it. It was like the turkeys mounted a counterattack! It was almost as if they were...*organized!!*

Mr. Carlson: *As God is my witness, I thought turkeys could fly.*

— WKRP in Cincinnati, Episode 8, 1978-1979

*   *   *   *   *

It's such a great line: *As God is my witness, I thought turkeys could fly!* In case you're wondering, turkeys–at least the Thanksgiving variety–generally can't.

It's 1978 and the first season of the new television comedy, "WKRP In Cincinnati". Some of us–especially those with slightly offbeat sense of humor–consider the episode "Turkeys Away" as one of the great moments in TV and comedy. It's also perhaps the world's greatest example–fictional or otherwise–of a massive business "Whoops!"

If you missed it (or are simply too young to remember), then here's the story in a nutshell: For a Thanksgiving Day promotion and to stage a brilliant marketing coup over their competitors, station manager Arthur Carlson conceives the idea of dropping live turkeys over a shopping mall from a helicopter as a giveaway promotion. Sounds good. But as the turkeys plummet to the ground, crashing through car windshields and windows, the scene is described by WKRP's on-site reporter, Les Nesman, as the reincarnation of the Hindenberg disaster! When all is said and done, Arthur sums it all up with the classic phrase, "As God is my witness, I thought turkeys could fly..."

A small miscalculation. Something he just never considered. Whoops!...

Success in anything, in life or in business is a *good* thing, a positive thing! Everyone will tell you that to succeed in anything you really need to have a positive attitude and outlook. I agree; that's absolutely true. The trouble with developing a positive attitude, however, is that you can start to believe that it's *not* okay to have a *negative* attitude, that is to look at all the things than can go wrong! I call it "Positive Blindness"! And that's how "Whoops!" happens–and one of the real Success "traps".

In years of working with business people, salespeople, and entrepreneurs, I see Positive Blindness a lot. The hardest thing is to ask these folks to do is to think about the reasons they might *not* be successful–what could go wrong with their plans, how their competitors might respond, what mistakes they may have made in their assumptions. Some of them can't do it or simply won't do it. It's just too painful and too scary. Almost like "if I look too hard at what can go wrong I might, God forbid, lose my positive attitude". It might burst the bubble of my great idea–and that's no fun!

Of course, nothing could be further from the truth. A real positive attitude, the kind that leads to real success, is one backed by confidence. Confidence comes from a combination of knowledge, experience, and having asked all the right questions, even the ones you didn't really want to hear the answers to.

When I first started my own business, I went to visit my friendly local banker for a business loan. I had a great business plan, not to mention an impressively written resume that would most certainly convince any doubting soul of my future success. That's when the bubble burst.

"What could go wrong?" asked the banker.

"Well, of course, I suppose there are lots of things but I feel what's important is to stay focused on the goal and be absolutely determined to achieve it", I answered.

"What will you do if things don't work out as you've planned?"

"I'll do whatever takes to be successful!"

"And why will you be successful where others have failed?"

"I am determined, I have great skills, and I am motivated!"

"What about your competition?"

"I'm better than they are!"

"And if you fail?…"

"I'll learn from my mistakes and move forward to success!"

It was quiet for a few minutes as we sat in her office. Finally she said, "You know, that might be enough to get you hired for a job at most companies, but it's not enough for us to invest a million dollars in your new business."

Obviously the woman lacked Vision…

The point? We'll call it the "Flying Turkeys Rule of Success":

The Right Plan is the one that succeeds when every possibility, positive and negative, has been considered and prepared for. The Plan works no matter what happens!

Success may contain "inspiration" and lots of "perspiration" but when all is said and done, it's mostly the result of "Preparation" and asking yourself the "hard questions".

Without it, that turkey just won't fly!

The Success Trap #2:

BE REALISTIC

"He's got his head in the clouds! That boy will never amount to anything!"

They said it about Thomas Edison. They said it about Henry Ford…and the Wright Brothers…about Einstein…and about thousands of others, many of whom can be counted among the world's greatest success stories. The Dreamers who imagined "the impossible" and yet somehow succeeded in making their dreams into reality.

But you say, "Edison and Einstein were geniuses, and the others probably were too!"

Maybe. And then again, maybe not. No one would argue that they were pretty bright guys but was that the root of their success? Maybe they just refused to let go of their dreams and listened to themselves, not everyone else!

When I was a young boy in the early '60's, my family moved to Denver, Colorado. My Dad was the new sales manager for a small local brewery, the Tivoli Brewing Company, and occasionally he would take me to work with him. The brewery was located downtown and a bit outside the "high rent district", so on the way we would pass along Larimer Street. In those days, Larimer Street was Denver's version of skid row (today it's one of Denver's showpieces). Early in the morning, the "bums" were still sleeping curled up against barred storefronts, a few early risers panhandling the business crowd.

With the naivetÈ that only a 10 year old can have, I asked him "How did all those bums get that way? Didn't they go to school?"

Dad answered, "Son, there are plenty of doctors and lawyers out there. All kinds of people including some pretty smart ones. For one reason or another they decided that they just couldn't make it." He didn't tell me how they got there exactly but I did figure out that ending up on Larimer Street didn't have a lot to do with education!

My friend, Jon, made what I thought was an amazingly insightful comment about people. He said "You really can't motivate people–they pretty much have to find that inside themselves; but you *can* DE-motivate them pretty easily!"

It's a funny aspect of human nature that we are so quick to believe it when others tell us we're wrong or that we can't accomplish something. That we're not being "realistic". Most of the time it comes from people who there's little reason to think know what they're talking about. It doesn't matter–it's still like it came from an Oracle on High. If someone…anyone…said it, then it must be true. Our response is to immediately doubt ourselves, perhaps even toss away our dreams or ideas all because someone said it wouldn't work.

Someone once said to me that I didn't dream big *enough*! I didn't know how to handle that either!

Maybe Edison and Einstein and Ford and all the rest were successful because they didn't listen to anyone but themselves. Maybe they didn't hear it when someone said, "Wilbur, my boy, be realistic. People can't fly!"

If you don't believe it, here's an easy test. Next time you have a personal success, big or small, call up everyone you know and tell them all about it. Tell them how excited you are. Brag a little! And watch what happens.

When I started my business I had some early good fortune. In the first year I did three times more business than I thought I could. I was feeling pretty good about it and couldn't resist telling friends and business associates about how well things were going–especially the ones who had been so supportive during the beginning struggle. I really expected that they would enjoy hearing about my success. Well, some did but most didn't.

I learned that it was easy to find lots of supporters when you're down or struggling, but my "tough times" supporters either didn't want to hear about my success or felt they should caution me not to get too cocky.

And do you know what my first, gut reaction was? That's right, it was "Maybe they're right! Maybe I was just lucky!" What kept me going was listening instead to the little voice deep down that said they weren't!

Who are you listening to? Dream BIG, avoid "Being Realistic", and have faith in your dreams.

The Success Trap #3:

"FAILURE IS A GREAT LEARNING EXPERIENCE!"

Don't you just love this one? "Failure is a great learning experience!" There's some truth here; you *can* learn some things when you fail. You can also *not learn* anything. There are folks who have failed, figured out what they did wrong and didn't do them again. That's good, I guess. There are also folks who failed and didn't learn anything. What went wrong? It seems like there should have been an easier way...

Is the implication of a "great learning experience" that everyone *should* fail? Does that mean that the smartest people are the ones who have failed over and over, and that they are now the best positioned for success (as long as they made different mistakes each time, I suppose)? No, I just think that "failure is a great learning experience" is about the only positive thing that you can say when you fail...or when you're trying to make someone feel better who has.

Let's be real. Failing stinks. Failure happens. Failing is the absolute pits. There is *nothing* worse. There is no 'feel good' way to justify it. People sometimes mess up. It's also not the end of the world, but that doesn't mean that it doesn't feel that way.

Yes, I have failed. I didn't particularly enjoy it and it cost me a lot of money. I *did* learn some things from it; mistakes that I would rather not repeat today. Looking back, however, I don't think that I could have done things differently than I did. At the time they seemed like good ideas–they weren't but they seemed that way! In other words, "Who knew?" I don't spend too much time thinking about all my mistakes. After all, there are so many that I still haven't made yet still waiting for me!

Failure is just the opposite side of the coin of Success. If there is no possibility of failing then there is equally no possibility of success. In fact, you could make the case that the higher you reach for success, the farther the possible fall to failure.

So what's a person to do? Always reach low?

May I offer some alternative thoughts and strategies on Failure?

When you have failed, you must immediately endeavor to do each of the following, perhaps over and over:

- kick yourself frequently and well—you probably deserve it.

- Blame yourself entirely unless you can absolutely prove beyond a shadow of a doubt that you had *nothing to do with it*. Do not blame anyone else.

- Experience the pain and disappointment—failing was not meant to be fun and satisfying.

- Make a list of all the stupid and wrong things you did. Read it frequently and irritate your friends with it. Hindsight is wonderful and you may as well try and learn *something* from it as long as you're here.

- Pretend you are a successful person and make fun of yourself. Be cruel! Very cruel…

- Resolve that you will never, never, never take risks again.

- Sleep curled up in your doorway with old clothes on. This will help you prepare for your eventual slide to skid row.

- Visit your friends and neighbors. Take a coffee cup with you, preferably tin, and ask them for their spare change. If you are unemployed this may not be a totally bad strategy…

- Recognize that you are wasting time doing all of the above when you could be getting on to something new and making a success of it…

The Success Trap #4:

"BUILD A BETTER MOUSETRAP"

Often the route to Success is generated by a "better idea". It could be a new product...or even *you!* I'm pretty sure that it was Ralph Waldo Emerson who said, *"Build a better Mousetrap and the world will beat a path to your door."* Ralph was wrong...really wrong...it simply doesn't work and it has left more than a few would-be successes scratching their heads and wondering what went wrong.

The problem isn't with the "build a better mousetrap" section. If you've got a great idea for a new product or service or a new design or way to do something then by all means go full speed ahead with it! Maybe you have an idea for starting a new business that meets a real need—if you can just get some funding and some customers. Maybe *you* are the better mouse-trap—you've worked hard and developed your skills, abilities, and perform-ance. You deserve some recognition and reward—like a promotion or salary increase. Your problem is that the world doesn't seem to be beating a "path to your door". What's wrong?

Maybe just this morning you asked yourself, "What is with those peo-ple (potential customers, the banker, your boss and co-workers, etc.)? Why can't they see a good idea when it's right in front of them?"

Let's suppose that you presented a really great idea to someone hoping for his or her encouragement, enthusiasm, or support and it seems like the light bulb just didn't go on for them. Maybe they even said, "I don't think that's such a good idea". So you're left wondering, "Why didn't they 'Get It'?"

Okay, let's see...what are the possible reasons they didn't "Get It"? By all means let's begin with the one that, being human, we're most likely to believe. They didn't "Get It" because "It's a really stupid idea!" (By the way, if they pointed out the 121 things that could go wrong with your idea or the insurmountable hurdles, that's pretty much a nice way of calling it "stupid").

In all fairness, "stupid idea" *is* always a possibility but it's actually not that likely. Your new "mousetrap" may go through a lot of changes and modifications before it becomes reality but chances are the core contains at least the beginnings of a pretty good idea. But again, being the humans that we are, you may have heard yourself uttering the phase that has no business in the vocabulary of any successful person:

"Yeah, you're probably right…"

I went to my town dump last weekend with a load of trash. It occurred to me that somewhere there must be a "dump" full of good ideas that got trashed because someone once called them stupid. I wish I could find it and mine it!

On the other hand, let's suppose that you refused to give up on your success idea just because you received a little negative comment. That's good. Instead you decided that your idea just needed more work and set about to perfect it. That's probably also good, unless you got stuck in *"The Search for the Perfect Mousetrap"*! You kept on working to improve and improve your "product" until it would become so perfect that no one would ever be able to criticize it. If only that were possible…either way your better mousetrap is in real danger of ending up on the trash heap.

Here are the three unassailable truths about better mousetraps and achieving Success.

First and foremost, not everybody will "Get It" no matter how hard you try, no matter how "perfect" the product. The challenge is to find the one's who probably will. In business it's called *target marketing*–finding your customer base, the one's who are most likely to need and appreciate what you have to offer. As for the others, just block your ears.

Second, use the **20/60/20 Rule** (It's served me well!): *In any group of people, 20% will think you're a genius and really "Get It"; 60% will consider what you have to say, think about I, and some will eventually "Get It"; and*

20% will think you're an idiot forever. Believe it! If you're getting 20/60/20 you're doing something right!

Third, and most important, you *have to learn how to Sell!*

I have a sign above my desk that says, "If they don't know about you they can't buy from you!" The world will never beat a path to your door unless you tell the world that you're there and how much you have to offer.

Bob is an engineer by training and years of experience. Last year Bob decided to go into business for himself as a consultant. He's developed an innovative software design process and toolset that software engineering firms should be knocking down his door for. But Bob still doesn't have any business and is about to give up.

"Bob", I said, "You've got to learn how to *sell* yourself, your products and your services. Get on the phone, make sales calls on companies and engineering people that you think you can sell to. Put together a powerful 'selling' website and a brochure. You've got to let people know that you've got a real winner to offer them! Remember what I said, 'If they don't know about you…'".

So what do you think Bob's response was?

"SELL????" cried Bob. *"I am NOT a salesman! I'm an engineer. Besides if what I have is good it should be clearly obvious."*

I suspect that Bob believes that "selling" is the task of getting people to do something or buy something that they wouldn't have done or bought otherwise. So having to *sell* his product is demeaning—and even suggests that he and his product have no real value!

Granted that in some circles Sales, unfairly I might add, might not be considered the most lustrous of professions, especially if it's defined that way. So let's try on a new definition of selling:

"SELLING" is the task of communicating with people to make SURE that your potential customer or audience absolutely, positively 'Get's It'"!

In other words, you just can't assume that what is obvious to you is obvious to someone else. If they figure it out on their own that's great, but by and large, it doesn't happen. It doesn't matter whether what you have to sell is yourself (for that raise or promotion), a product/service that you're offering, an idea that you want others to believe in, or an action you want someone to take. *Selling* is showing them *WHY* you believe in yourself, your idea, or your product–and what it can do for them!

Great salespeople can be found in all walks of life. Successful teachers, ministers, executives, and leaders of all kinds (and of course Salespeople). They actively "sell" their ideas–their "products" every day. Was Martin Luther King a great salesperson? How about Microsoft's Bill Gates? You bet!

In a journey to success, doing great things and waiting for the world to notice has never worked and never will.

The journey to Success only starts with a better mousetrap. It is the *continuous* selling that brings people down the path to your door! That's right, continuous! You've got to sell every single day if you want results!

Absolute truth!

"BE SMARTER THAN THE AVERAGE BEAR"

Assumption: Successful people are smart.

Assumption: The most successful people are the smartest!

Conclusion: It's important to act like you're confident and really smart if you want to be seen as successful.

Conclusion: Don't let anyone see you sweat!

"Smarter than the Av-er-age Bear!"–Yogi Bear

            *   *   *

In the mid-1970's and early 1980's I worked for Digital Equipment Corporation, at that time second only to IBM in the computer industry. Although DEC became part of Compaq Computer a few years ago, many of us who worked there in those years have fond memories of the company in its heyday. Few companies were better to work for or fostered greater creativity and independent thinking in their employees! All in all, a great place to work and to learn.

I had just come from a field sales position into corporate headquarters as a new sales training manager, and worked in a division headed by Stan Olsen, one of DEC's two founders. Ken and Stan Olsen conceived and started DEC. Ken became President and CEO and Stan a Senior Vice President.

Now, Ken Olsen was a dynamic and forceful leader. A powerful motivator. He seemed to always know what he wanted and how to achieve it.

He was bigger than life; the man who was leading all of us to success. Frankly, everyone was pretty much in awe of Ken.

Stan was different. An engineer by profession, I remember Stan as quiet, a listener–a man who considered everything carefully before he made a decision. Stan didn't always seem to have a lot to say but he asked a lot of questions. "What are you doing? Why are you doing it this way?" When I once told Stan about a problem we were dealing with, I was amazed when he asked *me*, "What do you think we should do?"

Who was the smarter, the more successful of the Olsen brothers? That's a patently unfair question. Still, as much as I admired Ken (and still do), I always gave the edge to Stan. Ken was clearly the visionary and the leader but Stan did one thing that I felt made him stand above: *he surrounded himself with brilliance.*

Stan Olsen didn't *have* to be brilliant in his own right (although he certainly was). His real brilliance was in how he developed a team of incredibly talented and brilliant Vice Presidents and continuously "mined" their intelligence and ideas. Stan and his VP's pioneered new products, opened new markets, and designed new concepts for DEC that in many respects set the tone for the technology marketplace of today. And last I heard, each of his VP's went on to outstanding careers of his own.

Being successful–in life or in business–is too often confused with personal *brilliance*. Success it seems goes to the smartest, the hardest working, the "leaders", the movers and the shakers, the ones with all the answers. "If you want people to see you as a success, act confident–never let them know you don't have all the answers!"

Well, I don't know about you but if experience has taught me anything it's that I have very few of the answers! I wish I had them all but, plain and simple, I don't–and obviously I'm willing to admit it! I do have lots and lots of ideas but I've also proven that more of them are clunkers than diamonds! I should also mention that I'm not all that good at acting like I have all the answers either (my wife sees through me on a regular basis).

What I am pretty good at, though, is *Mining*. I look for advice, opinion, and ideas everywhere. I find them in the newspaper and magazines, in overheard conversations on airplanes and restaurants, from my competitors, from my friends, from partnerships and alliances I've developed, from my customers–and, of course from my wife and family! The thing is, I probably disagree with what I hear far more than I agree, but that's okay. It's the continual input of ideas that let's me *learn* and makes me *think*, that helps me create my own ideas and success strategies (the ones that work!), and test them to see if they'll actually fly.

When I first started my own business, I began an *Idea Bank*. An Idea Bank was a place that I would record every good idea I came across–mine or someone else's. The account will never be full but it's become so packed with ideas that it's paying dividends on a regular basis.

What's the bottom line? You don't have to be brilliant to be successful. You don't have to be smarter than everyone else to be the *most* successful. You do have to be willing to *learn*.

Oh by the way, never tell anyone that you listened to anyone else or got an idea from anywhere except your own head. After all, it's important to maintain that "I'm smarter that the average bear" image!

The Success Trap #6:

"NO ONE SAID IT WAS SUPPOSED TO BE FUN!"

Why not? Why shouldn't the journey to success be incredibly fun all the time? Who said you have to work hard to be successful? Is there a connection between *fun* and *success*?

We're getting into some tricky territory here. This trap sounds like some serious heresy! Can you *not* work hard and still be successful, short of winning the lottery?

Did you ever notice the guy at work who is always the first to arrive in the morning and the last to leave? Everybody always says, *"Man, that Jack really puts the hours in!"* If you've noticed "Jack" then you may have noticed that he's not necessarily the most successful person in the company. Hard work doesn't guarantee success.

Who *is* the most successful and what do people say about *them*?

"He/She's really good and makes it look so easy!"

Those *successful people* always look like they're having *fun*. You would think they would look exhausted but instead they seem to be filled with energy and enthusiasm…Strange…

"Well, success will do that for you!"

I wonder if successful people were serious and exhausted before they were successful? Were they then magically transformed? Did *fun* just appear once they had "made it"?

"Who ever said that work (or Life) was supposed to be Fun?"

It's odd, but almost every really successful person I have ever know says that they actually had *more fun* on the way to Success than once they actually reached their goals. Makes you wonder if having fun has something to do with achieving success.

A college student told me that he was a majoring in business and planning to go on for an MBA. I said, "That's great. You must really enjoy Business!" He answered, "Not really. I'd rather do something else but Business is where the money is. I'll enjoy the money!"

If the most successful people found more enjoyment "in the journey than the destination" then maybe the college student has the cart before the horse because I expect he's not going to enjoy the trip.

My daughter asked me what I thought she should do in life. What should she major it, what career should she pursue. I said, "Figure out what you like to do more than anything else–the absolute most fun thing you can think of–and go for that!" She thought for a while and told me that she loved doing illustrations and artwork.

"But, Dad, who would want to hire me for that? It doesn't seem like I could make a lot of money either."

"Try thinking of it this way," I said. "If you're really having fun doing something, the chances are that you will become exceptionally good at it. If you're really good, success…and money…will take care of themselves."

Consider the converse: people who are not doing something that they really love tend to find very little "fun" in it. They rarely, if ever, become real "top performers" with the success/money it brings. And those that "gut it out" and actually do get to the top, too often find they don't enjoy their success nearly as much as they thought they would (if the journey didn't kill them first).

"Dan" was determined to get to the top of IBM. He and his wife often spoke about how you "have to make some sacrifices along the way" if you're going to make it. Together they endured relocations and uprooting of their family every couple of years, good and not-so-good assignments, long days and nights, and company politics. But "Dan" progressed steadily ahead one promotion after another.

"Dan" never made to the top of IBM although he came very close. In the end, he was just in the wrong position at the wrong time when a corporate restructuring eliminated his position. Not his fault really–a miscalculation. Just one of those things that happens. Shortly thereafter, a new opportunity opened for Dan outside of IBM, one that brought him even more success than he had planned for. "Still," his friends said, "you must have been crushed when IBM fell through for you after all your hard work." "What hard work?" answered Dan. "We had a great time and besides everything worked out–just not exactly the way we planned!"

Just so there's no confusion, hard work will always be a component of success. When the work is *fun*, however, I question the use of the word *hard*. I work a great deal and I have put a lot of effort into making my life and my business a success. But did I work "hard"? I know that it's a matter of semantics, but to me "hard" implies doing work that you don't really enjoy–and I certainly have not had much of that!

If you're not having Fun, maybe you're working too hard!!

The Success Trap #7:

"SUCCESS IS A NEW MERCEDES!"

Everyone defines success on his or her own terms—and that's about the only way you will ever find it. When you define it on someone else's terms or expectations it becomes elusive at best, unsatisfying at its worst.

What does "the world" say success is? The big house with a new Mercedes in the driveway? A big bank account? Recognition and status? Beauty, fame, security, happiness? Holding a top company position?

It's not what the world says that matters. Success can be *anything* you want it to be. It is whatever *you* define it to be. It's what works for you and only you! Success should be whatever makes you incredibly happy and that you're willing to strive for. The problems arise when we confuse what we think we really want with what we're told we *should* want.

We've all heard the stories of "successful" people who, after accumulating riches and power, were still not happy. (I personally have often wept for them contemplating the depths of their misery.) I have to think that the only possible explanation is that what they achieved wasn't actually "success"! It looked liked success, walked like success, but once they got it, it wasn't what they really wanted.

So it's confusing...*what do I really want from life?* There are so many mixed messages. It seems like everyone is telling you what you should want or what you should aspire to. How on earth do you figure out what's right for you?

It's especially easy to confuse success with accumulating *things* (like a new Mercedes). Success really doesn't have a lot to do with things. It's much more about achieving a certain quality of life that makes you happy—which could, of course, include having lots and lots of really great things! But it doesn't have to.

When you really get down to it, success for most people is ultimately about achieving and perfecting one or more of *The Four Life Values…Power, Fame, Relationships, and Safety.*

The Four Life Values

Power–

Power is all about Control, Achievement, and Status. "Power People" seek and value more control of the world around them. It may be having control of his or her own lives and destinies; it may be gaining "positional control" as a leader or manager in a corporate or organizational setting. Control is important because it enables that person to aggressively move to achieve whatever objectives he or she may have. Equally as important as achieving goals, is status and recognition. "Power" wants to be tangibly and publicly recognized for what he or she achieves and measured against others. So money, position, home, auto, or other "trappings" of power are important visible measures of success.

"Power" is also a planner and a decision maker. He or she will take moderate, considered risks when he or she is confident that all necessary information has been gathered and that outcomes and options have been considered. "Power's" goals then are aggressive, but most importantly realistic and achievable and he or she views life in the black and white terms of "winning and losing".

Fame–

Fame is about *Applause.* "Fame People" live for *Achievement, Recognition* and the *Approval* of those around them–their audience. "Fame" dreams the great dreams, and may set lofty one-chance-in-a-million goals. "Fame" is accused of *flying by the seat of the pants* because he or she often resists details and planning and prefers to make decisions on intuition, creative ideas, and feelings. "Fame" is a great risk-taker because only great risks can bring great rewards. The strong possibility of failure always exists but "Fame" stays focused on the dream.

Fame is an on-stage, "Star" personality because achievement without recognition is not really success. The physical trappings of success may be unimportant. What is important, however, is the immediate response and positive feedback of those around them.

"Fame" may be an entrepreneur in business. He or she loves the unstructured, creative, high-risk environment of a start-up. Unpredictability and change are positives, not negatives because they challenge "Fame's" ability to overcome unanticipated obstacles. For exactly these reasons "Fame" may not be as successful in a structured corporate environment.

Relationships–

"Relationship People" value exactly that: their *Relationships* with *People*. Mutual positive *Feelings* are most important as well as the give and take of thoughts, ideas, concerns, and emotions. Honesty, caring, and openness are highly valued as well as the importance of family.

"Relationship" is a *caregiver* and may often put other's feelings or needs above his or her own. Decisions should be made by consensus; confrontation should be avoided unless there is no other option. Success is measured by the strengths of the relationships he or she builds and maintains. Relationship" will take moderate risks but only when he is confident that a decision or action is beneficial to others.

"Relationship" people are often drawn to human-service professions that value their strong abilities for one-on-one interaction and focus upon feelings and interpersonal relationships.

Safety–

"Safety People" generally value *Predictability* and *Security* above all else. "Safety" likes to deal with facts and values orderly processes, "Safety" is generally risk-averse unless he or she is convinced of a compelling reason or that all possible outcomes have been fully considered and prepared for.

Not surprisingly, "Safety" people may often be drawn to positions and careers that are process driven and utilize facts and figures to generate highly predictable results. Engineering, information technology, finance and accounting—all reflect "Safety's attention to detail and data.

Just as "Fame" can be blindly optimistic, "Safety" runs the risk of pessimism and the assumption that the "glass is always half-empty". "Safety" may view Success is the reduction of risk and maintenance of the status quo.

Most people have a mix of these Life Values and have a broader mix of success goals. For example, "Fame" may be focused on achieving stardom but not at the expense of his or her family and friends. What we do know is that each of us ultimately determines our personal definition of Success from our unique mix of Life Goals—unless we make the mistake of letting others define our success.

Take a look again at the Four Life Values. "Power" and "Relationship" are in many respects opposites, as are "Fame" and "Safety". Neither is good or bad but they value vastly different things. So who is "whispering in your ear" and telling you how you should define success? It doesn't matter if it's your spouse, your parents, your boss, or a well-meaning friend. What they're telling you is colored by their Life Values, not necessarily yours! It's one case where opposites do not attract!

In other words, "Consider the Source!"

Success is not always a new Mercedes!

AM I ON TRACK FOR SUCCESS?

Okay, let's suppose that you now have a pretty good idea of what you want from life and your personal path to Success. Here are a few final thoughts…a short personal "test" to see if your Success Goal is really right for you and if you're on track today.

- What do you really want? Power, Fame, Relationship, or Safety? Will the Success Goal that you have set for yourself give you what you really need? Did you set the goal or did you listen to "other voices"?

- Will getting there be is as much fun as being there? We're back to that *fun* thing again but it's really the key to everything. If you're not having fun then why are you doing it?

- Will it take hard work to achieve? It might be *lots* of *difficult* work, but it shouldn't be *hard work*.

- Will it pass the "Stupid Idea" test? Do you believe in yourself and what you want enough that you can weather the "nay Sayers"?

- Can you stay on track when your idea of success doesn't match other people's—or what others tell you it *should* be?

- Can you create a Plan, a step-by-step action plan that will get you where you want to go?

- Do you know how you'll keep going even when your plan doesn't work out exactly the way you thought it would? Can you "blow off" *failure* as just a minor setback—and still keep going?

- Are you willing to listen and learn, use every possible resource? Have the humility to know that no one, least of all you, has all the answers?

- Are you ready to *SELL* the entire world if necessary to gain the Success you want?

Then go for it!…

THE IDEA BANK...AND HOW TO FIND GREAT IDEAS FOR SUCCESS

Success is never achieved in a vacuum. If we take the time to look and listen we come across great success ideas every day. Ideas that motivate...or solve a problem...or open a new opportunity for success. Thoughts for my personal "Idea Bank" have come from every imaginable source–books and newspapers, television, great speakers, business associates, friends and family. Occasionally they even come from me! An idea occurs to me at night, while waiting for an airplane or driving in the car.

Sometimes great ideas are just what you need right then. More often they're an idea that you want to keep for future reference...maybe a motivational thought that you would like to keep in mind.

I used to write all these great ideas I came across on scraps of paper or on the backs of business cards. Not too surprisingly I promptly lost most of them. Actually they're probably still hidden deep in one of my desk drawers but that's the "black hole of Calcutta"–once in and never to be seen again! Hence the Idea Bank...a simple place to store and find your wealth of Great (and even not-so-great) Ideas. You'll find a simple but effective Idea Bank to get you started in the next section of this book.

I do have a lot of ideas. As I've said, there are a lot of clunkers but fortunately a few great ones that have really paid off. Again, you just can't have too many ideas. Even the clunkers can teach you something. When I need a good idea (and that's most of the time!) I've always found that the best approach is to go for volume and then mine through them looking for a good one. Of course it helps if you've got a lot of ideas to begin with.

My friend and business associate, Jonathan Narducci, once asked me, *"Where do you get all of your ideas? Every time we talk you come up with some new ideas to get new business or for a new program!"*

"That's easy," I answered. *"From you."*

"Me?"

"Sure," I said. *"I listen to what you say, then I think about it, add some of my own thoughts, and Voila! A New Idea!"* (Remember, I never said they were all *great* ideas!)

"Do I get paid for my contribution?" asked Jon.

"No."

Create an Idea Factory

Do you want to generate some great ideas of your own? Do a little creative thinking? Then create an *Idea Factory*.

Think of it like a manufacturing process. You have to begin with *Raw Materials*. So get started by collecting lots of thoughts and ideas in your personal *idea bank*. You can't have too much raw material! The more you have, the greater your capability to produce something great.

Now move to the Preparation step. Think about the challenges you face and what you're trying to achieve. Read through your idea bank. Don't look to find an exact solution there (although it's fine if you do!) but just browse to remember what's inside and to fill up your *idea hopper.*

Now it's time to start the *Processing* step. This is the tricky part because there's nothing you can really do that will start ideas immediately spewing out. Creative thinking is mostly a function of the subconscious mind. The subconscious works pretty much autonomously–pose a problem to it, fill it with enough raw materials, sit back and let it work. It does work and it will if you give it a chance.

We're not done yet! We still have the *Output Process* ahead. Believe it or not, your subconscious is working and ideas are starting to flow–but you'll miss them unless you *take* time and *make* time to *Listen*!

I make "idea time" for myself almost every morning. The kids leave for school at 7:30AM and the house (and my home office) are quiet. 7:30 to 8:30 is my idea time. I sit down with a cup of coffee and a notepad, turn on "Good Morning America" and spend an hour or so *listening and thinking*. I think about the day ahead, the projects I'm working on, review my "to do's" and pose problems to myself–*How could I do this better? Where could I find some new business? Is there another way to do this that's more efficient and effective?* Then I listen to myself–and write down whatever comes to me. Sometimes there's a gold mine of ideas and sometimes not much at all. That's okay; ideas come at their own speed–maybe I need to put a little more in the "idea hopper" to increase production!

Idea Time for you might be on the way to work, in the evening before bed, or any other time that you can at least be by yourself. Many of my best ideas pop up during a solo lunch or dinner when I'm traveling. On an airplane works pretty well for me too, or in a hotel room during a business trip. Whatever works for you.

Give it a try!

THE IDEA BANK

Date: _____
Source:_____
Idea:_____
_____
_____
_____

Date: _____
Source:_____
Idea:_____
_____
_____
_____

Date: _____
Source:_____
Idea:_____
_____
_____
_____

Date: _____
Source:_____
Idea:_____
_____
_____
_____

Date: _____

Source:_____

Idea:_____

_____

_____

_____

_____

Date: _____

Source:_____

Idea:_____

_____

_____

_____

_____

Date: _____

Source:_____

Idea:_____

_____

_____

_____

_____

Date: _____

Source:_____

Idea:_____

_____

_____

_____

_____

Date: _____

Source:_____

Idea:_____

_____

_____

_____

Date: _____

Source:_____

Idea:_____

_____

_____

_____

Date: _____

Source:_____

Idea:_____

_____

_____

_____

Date: _____

Source:_____

Idea:_____

_____

_____

_____

Date: _____

Source:_____

Idea:_____

_____

_____

_____

Date: _____

Source:_____

Idea:_____

_____

_____

_____

Date: _____

Source:_____

Idea:_____

_____

_____

_____

Date: _____

Source:_____

Idea:_____

_____

_____

_____

Date: _____

Source:_____

Idea:_____

_____

_____

_____

Date: _____

Source:_____

Idea:_____

_____

_____

_____

Date: _____

Source:_____

Idea:_____

_____

_____

_____

Date: _____

Source:_____

Idea:_____

_____

_____

EPILOGUE

So tell me this, what other career could have been this challenging or this much fun?

Perhaps in the final analysis, selling isn't about all the traditional reasons for doing it, such as "big money" or promotion potential. The sales pros know that there is no challenge in business or any other profession that even comes close to equaling selling. Hard work, creativity, understanding people, developing internal motivation, achievement, and even failure…they're all just part of our world.

And who else can say that?

ABOUT THE AUTHOR

Tim McMahon is the bestselling author of three sales and management books including *Selling 2000, Solving the Sales Management Equation,* and his most recent, *The Success Traps–The 7 Fatal Traps on the Journey to Success.*

He is a respected futurist on "21st Century Selling and frequent keynote speaker at international conferences and corporate sales meetings. He consults to leading worldwide corporations on Business Success Strategies, Value Selling, Sales & Management Development, Knowledge Management (KM) and CRM/Sales Automation strategies.

McMahon is the publisher of "The Value Proposition" e-magazine that reaches thousands of sales & management professionals in 25 countries.

Tim McMahon has more than 30 years of outstanding experience and accomplishment in Sales and Management with IBM, Digital Equipment, and Dun+Bradstreet, and as a highly successful business entrepreneur. He is a professional member of the National Speakers Association and is the developer of "Strategy Mapping".

At the National Sales Management Conference, he was recognized as "*one of the world's Top Three Experts in Sales and Management*".

Tim McMahon's articles and commentary have appeared in Fortune, The Wall Street Journal, and numerous other major publications and he has appeared on CNN and CNBC International. He recently completed a televised special for *The Computer Channel* on 21st Century Selling and Customer Relationship Management.

He is the publisher of the leading international sales E-Magazine, "The Value Proposition"

Tim McMahon and his family reside in New Hampshire.

For more information and sales resources, visit Tim's web site at www.mcmahonworldwide.com

0-595-22268-4